Joanne M Amt '/2019

THE PRICE NEGOTIATION PLAYBOOK

A Practical B2B Guide for
Winning Your Best Price with Confidence

JOANNE M. SMITH
Author of *The Pricing and Profit Playbook*

Bradley Publishing

Bradley Publishing: 122 Hartefeld Drive, Avondale, Pennsylvania 19311

First Edition. Printed in the United States.
ISBN 978-0-9897238-2-4
Library of Congress Control Number: 2018902859

Editor: Jeanne Marie Blystone
Cover design and interior layout by Kerrie Lian,
under contract with Karen Saunders and Associates:
www.KarenSaundersAssoc.com

To my extended family, for your love and support.
Each of you enrich my life.

Contents

Introduction: Transforming Your Price Negotiations

Businesses big and small are always looking for ways to give their sales teams an edge in the marketplace. Many invest in programs to hone sales negotiation skills such as mastering the conversation, understanding the customer's needs, overcoming resistance, building relationships, preparing for the negotiation, and finally, closing the deal. While these skills are crucial, they only amount to half the story. Equally important is the art and science of price negotiation—how to make smart price decisions that will help close the deal and do it at a fair price. The very best companies know that the ability to effectively negotiate—to close the deal at the right price—is the number one skill for success in today's competitive business environment.

Why is price negotiation important? Because pricing has never been more critical and challenging than it is now. Companies are facing emerging low-priced competitive imports, low-priced local competition that seems to pop up overnight, and low-priced online channels which are eroding market prices. At the same time, buyers are getting more sophisticated and aggressive with their price-pressure tactics.

The best sales negotiation books and training courses available today don't address most of the key issues in price negotiation. They introduce the concept of insisting on a price premium for value, yet they often don't address how to determine the amount of the price premium. Others touch on small aspects of pricing, but none explore the full scope of skills needed to truly reach a fair and maximum price time after time. Almost always, the actions or potential actions of aggressive competitors are not addressed. And far too often, they ignore how the actions of individual salespeople can combine to create a more aggressive marketplace. Of Amazon's top 100 selling 'negotiation books' and top 100 'sales books' only five books dedicated a chapter to price negotiation—most with three pages or less.

When sales representatives are predominantly encouraged or incented to grow volume, they are delighted with higher close rates often achieved with discounting. However, business owners should be wary because the odds are great that profits lie far more in price performance than volume performance. In fact, for the average Fortune 1000 company, pricing is four times as powerful in increasing profits as volume! In the more than one hundred businesses I have guided through price decisions, I found initial evidence, in nearly all of them, of pricing or promotional decisions that drove volume increases which *reduced* their earnings. They were celebrating higher volume without realizing they had destroyed earnings. Often these sales resources, or marketing resources in the case of promotions, are held up as heroes within their company for their outstanding growth performance. Their personal compensation increases, yet the unseen hidden truth is they often have destroyed profits.

In business-to-business (B2B) companies, missed opportunities in pricing often account for 5%–10% revenue loss which could translate into a 50%–100% lost earning opportunity. That's the equivalent of a $1 billion revenue business—with $200 million in pre-tax earnings—missing out on up to $100 million in revenue that flows to $100 million in earnings.

Further Evidence of Weak Price Negotiation Skills

- A study by Christian Homburg, Institute for Market-Oriented Management found over 80% of companies believe their prices are higher than their competitors![1] Impossible, we can't all be higher! If you believe your price is higher than competition, there is a good chance that buyers will push you to a lower price than you deserve.

- Simon-Kucher & Partners consistently found approximately 60% of B2B companies thought they were in a price war, yet approximately 90% thought the other guy started it![2] Again, impossible. Businesses do not realize how their own behaviors influence the market price.

I am a strong advocate for sales negotiation training, but don't assume you have gained strong *price* negotiation skills in these courses. *Price* negotiation skills are every bit as important as *sales* negotiation skills. They must go hand-in-hand if you want superior profits.

My Playing Experience

I led the pricing transformation of the DuPont company from a time when DuPont had no formal pricing focus, and other then a few pockets of strength, had mediocre performance. In the early days and months, I heard consistent messages from the DuPont sales organizations across over 50 diverse businesses and across every region in the world: "*We can't raise price—our market is too competitive! Our competitors will not follow us and we will lose our volume!*" or "*We had to significantly discount that customer (and that one and that one) to keep their volume.*" Our sales force was very experienced yet very skeptical about our ability to raise price. Overtime, with training and practice, that skepticism turned to conviction. They were amazed at their own success.

During the time I was leading price, DuPont went from a $28 billion revenue company to an over $35 billion company.

A look at the previous decade of pricing showed times when the market dynamics were favorable (e.g., rising raw materials) and times where the market was unfavorable (e.g., recessions). Yet overall, there had been a steady decline in pricing, and along with it, a steady decline in DuPont's contribution margin. I'm proud to say we turned that performance around and we did it quickly. Over the next seven years, we successfully increased price, quarter after quarter for 24 out of 26 fiscal quarters. (See figure I.1). We even increased price two of the four quarters in the 2009 recession delivering over $200 million in pricing profits for the year. Most other years' profits rose nearly $1 billion from pricing efforts.

Figure I.1 DuPont Year-Over-Year Quarterly Price Increase History

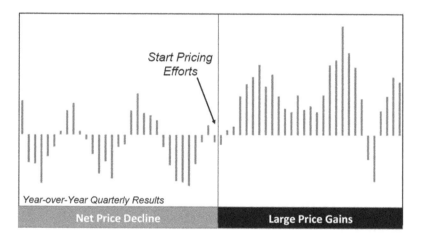

This pricing success was due to better price negotiations along with improvements in our pricing strategies, culture, organization, processes, and systems. However, the best price-setting strategies only bring a company so far. In the end, sales must execute the price. In my experience, half of any business's success comes from setting price strategies and half comes from strong execution. During this time at Du-

Pont, we continued to build the pricing execution skills of our sales force, leaders, and pricing resources. Initially, we used external firms to lead training courses, but as our experience developed I brought that training in-house. Over time, I developed new practical tools and practices to further enhance the training effectiveness.

A few years into our pricing journey, I was asked to take on the additional responsibility of starting up and leading DuPont's Customer Loyalty Initiative. Some readers may find it unusual that DuPont would elect to have customer loyalty led by the same person who leads pricing. On the surface, these two areas might appear at odds; increasing prices upsets customers which can only hurt customer loyalty. However, they are not. In fact, our businesses with the highest customer loyalty scores were typically the businesses with the highest pricing success. We had periods where we went from very low price increases to high price increases and our loyalty score rose 30%. Here's the good news: the pricing principles and practices shared in this book are all about achieving your fair price, not about taking unfair advantage of your customers. The very foundation of good pricing is trust and fairness. Fairness is relative to your value; the more value your customer perceives, the higher your pricing should be. The foundation of customer loyalty works similarly. Create value and it leads to trust and fairness.

In 2013, I started Price to Profits Consulting. I have worked with a vast array of companies including BASF, GE, Evonik, Huntsman, SABIC, Westlake Chemicals, Air Liquide, GAF Roofing, and Lennox Industries, as well as small privately held companies. Some of these companies have long-standing pricing organizations while others have none. Just like DuPont, most of these businesses started the conversation with, "*Our business is different because...*"

What I found may surprise you. There is far more commonality than difference in these diverse businesses. From business and sales leaders, I often hear, *"Sales has no confidence to hold or raise price. They think they must discount to get the business."* From sales organizations, I address many of the following common statements:

- *"I can't raise price; my market is too competitive!"*

- *"Our competitors have lower price."*

- *"We have tried to increase price, but competitors won't follow."*

- *"We have tried to increase price, but my customers will not accept the increase."*

I have a different view on their challenges. The odds are extremely high that it is the result of certain unrecognized behaviors—from leaders and sales—that are undermining their confidence and ability to gain price. Fortunately, these behaviors can be changed. Here are a few high-level examples of results from my training workshops and consulting engagements to illustrate this point:

- A highly skeptical $1 billion business unit with declining profits raised price quickly and successfully to achieve over $25 million in profit increase.

- Another business, $1.5 billion in sales, had just increased price with moderate success immediately before attending training. After the training workshop, they surprised themselves by implementing yet another increase with higher success, achieving an additional $30 million in profit increase.

- A business which suffered with low success rates in their annual price increase more than doubled their price increase success.

- A company, which announced consecutive price increases over five plus years, yet showed declining actual prices, successfully implemented a price increase with confidence and success.

The common denominator in all these cases was the realization by each business's sales organization that they had more pricing power than they realized and their own sales and/or leadership behaviors had been hurting pricing. This combined with new skill sets and confidence allowed them to significantly improve their price and profits.

One final note about my background: I have extensive experience in product-line and business management as well as operations. I understand that for you, as sales leaders and professionals, pricing is not your only focus. You are juggling volume growth, pricing, and customer loyalty, all while trying to keep your internal costs at a manageable level. No worries. The advice in this book balances these critical business levers to optimize your profits today while creating a lasting profitable business.

The Structure of This Playbook

There are many parallels between achieving a winning football season and achieving a winning pricing season. Both require excellence in offensive plays, defensive plays, and special plays. So, throughout this book I use sports analogies to illustrate the key concepts for price negotiations.

This B2B playbook for sales professionals, sales leaders, and pricing resources is divided into four sections that present the "Plays" essential for transforming weak price negotiations into superior price negotiations with a focus on practical, easy approaches. I have added tools that sales personnel can use going forward to reinforce the course material and allow them to easily practice what they learned. While best practice 'offensive moves' for raising price and 'defensive moves' for minimizing price discounts are put in place, the most effective decisions will combine offensive and defensive learnings. Each play builds on the play before it, so ultimately you will gain a comprehensive skill set along with a comprehensive toolbox (✖) that allows you to turn these complex choices into easy, simple, and smart decisions.

Play 1: The Foundation of Pricing Negotiations: The foundational elements needed for smart decisions focus on the four forces that influence the market price and price/volume trade-off decisions. Whether increasing price, holding price, or considering price drops, it is essential to employ these foundational elements.

Play 2: The Skills for Fair Price and Price Increase Negotiations: Smart offensive skills can double or triple your price increase success rate. They include the 'special plays' to ensure you will get fairly paid for your value and the skills that encourage higher market prices.

Play 3: The Skills for Smart Price-Drop Decisions: In the B2B world, there is almost always some level of discounting, or in the case of price increases, some level of price increase relief. Specific skills for recognizing when you have pricing power with different buyer types, knowing how to minimize the amount and frequency of price discounts, and learning how to manage aggressive competitors are instrumental to success.

Play 4: The Skills for Balancing Growth, Customer Loyalty, & Price: There are smart ways to grow without reverting to dropping price. Building customer loyalty results in price premiums and volume growth. A simple and practical approach to creating your growth strategy can help gain share without relying on discounting.

The Game Plan: Courage, Confidence, and Conviction

The ultimate goal of this book is to significantly increase courage, confidence, and conviction in achieving your fair price as well as in influencing the market price to higher levels. You will develop the skills to fully utilize your pricing power; to know when to go for a touchdown or a field goal and when you need to punt.

Confidence arises from the framework below which is the guiding principle of this book:

- **Fair Price:** Believing your price (or price increase) is fair

- **Committed Leadership:** Believing your leadership is fully committed to getting your fair price

- **Skills:** Having the necessary skills to negotiate successfully

Let the games begin.

PLAY 1:
PRICE EXECUTION
FUNDAMENTALS

Winning game after game, or negotiation after negotiation, requires understanding the fundamentals of the game—both offensive and defensive. Players need to recognize how their actions affect the opposing players on the field and what that likely reaction will be. They need to integrate that understanding with how their own behaviors affect the performance of their team and how each play can affect future plays. In short, mastering the fundamentals leads to more touchdowns and less turnovers.

Over time you'll experience favorable market dynamics which allow for the opportunity to raise price. You'll also go through difficult or unfavorable market dynamics causing downward pricing pressure. Yet, on a smaller scale, sales reps are facing these dynamics—customer by customer—on a routine basis, thus the need for both offensive and defensive skills.

Some sales resources mistakenly assume that their actions have no bearing on the rest of the sales team. These very salespeople believe their actions with each customer are 'secret' and will not affect the overall market dynamics. The truth is that every salesperson's actions positively or negatively affect the market dynamics and the market price.

The same holds true—perhaps more so—for your leadership. Leadership sets the pricing strategy and the tone that guides the sales teams. If they don't understand pricing fundamentals, they are undoubtedly and unintentionally having a negative impact on the market price. The best leaders consciously behave in ways that encourage upward pressure on the market price.

Sales are continually faced with price/volume trade-offs. *Should you go for volume, giving up price to do so? Should you go for fair price and risk losing all or a piece of the account?* Many salespeople—as well as their leadership—fumble these trade-off decisions often destroying potential profits and likely contributing to a more aggressive marketplace. These decisions are far from intuitive—for most readers the best price/volume trade-off decision is likely to be shockingly different than your expectation.

You, along with your leaders, must understand these dynamics as they are the essential foundation to everything else that follows in this playbook.

Chapter 1:
The Four Forces for Influencing the Market Price

Let's begin with the myth: *"The market sets the price—we can't influence the market price."* This is a dangerous and costly belief. If you believe it, you are never going to take the appropriate proactive actions that contribute to upward pricing pressure. You are also likely to take actions that inadvertently contribute to a much more aggressive marketplace with lower prices for all players. That is how to lose the pricing and profit game.

Think of it as pushing a large rock uphill. If you stop pushing, it will roll back down the hill. There is no neutral position. You are either pushing against gravity or gravity is pushing you down. Likewise, you are either proactively working to influence the market price higher or you are having a negative impact on the market price. Whether you are interested in holding your price, conservatively increasing your price, or boldly increasing your price, you must adopt daily behaviors that put upward pressure on the market price.

The four forces that affect an industry's market price are your competitors, your customers, yourselves, and market dynamics. (See Figure 1.1.) Leveraging these four forces is truly the foundation for strong price negotiations. While this is especially true for large and mid-sized companies, even the behaviors of small companies can result in lower market price. In highly fragmented industries, it is more of a challenge, yet influencing customers is essential.

Figure 1.1. The Four Market Forces for Price Execution Success

Force 1: The Competitive Force

Let's assume we all agree that 99.9% of the time having a higher market price is a good thing that will lead to higher prices and profits for you. It will also lead to higher prices for your competitors. Thus far, I've been making analogies to sports. However, when it comes to market price, this is one place that the win-lose concept of playing sports is the wrong concept. When it comes to market price, you need to think about a win-win concept as it relates to your competitors. A win-lose strategy leads to price wars. You drop price to gain share—your competitors respond by dropping their price to regain share, and the downward pricing spiral begins. In the end, the only winners are the customers with lower prices. All competitors end up with lower prices and lower profits— a lose-lose game.

There is an analogy here to the well-known "prisoner's dilemma."[3] The prisoner's dilemma occurs when two individuals act in ways that support their own best interests at the expense of each other, but it ultimately works to their disadvantage. For example, two criminals are being interrogated, separately, by the police. The police use their best tactics to convince each criminal that the first criminal who confesses will get the better deal. The police imply that the other criminal is already confessing. Each criminal is now uncertain of their partner-in-crime's actions. They try to protect themselves by confessing first. As a result, both criminals go to jail. Had the criminals maintained their silence, they would have both gone free. In the pricing analogy, the buyer is using his best tactics to convince each supplier that their price is higher than competition and they must lower their price or risk losing their volume. Often one of the suppliers falls into this trap—allowing this uncertainty to undermine their confidence. This supplier drops price to protect their volume. Before long, other suppliers are dropping price as well. The suppliers end up with lower profits than if they had stayed committed to their fair price (or their fair price increase).

Every time you enter a negotiation, you are setting a pricing game plan—intentionally or unintentionally. *Should you drop price to gain share? Raise price to gain profits?* Your decision is likely based on what you believe your competitor will do. *Will they drop price in an attempt to take your share?* The more convinced you are that your competition will or might drop their price, the more likely you are to drop your price. *So how do you know what play your competition is going to call?*

Likely you'd rely on past behavior as the best indicator of future behavior; and likely, you'd be right. Just be aware that recent management changes can result in different, unexpected behaviors. Additionally, human nature leads us to focus more on negatives rather than positives, thus you may have a natural bias towards assuming the worst; competitors will drop price. Let's examine three scenarios:

- If, historically, your competitor tends to use price to gain share, you are likely to believe they will or might drop price in a similar situation.

- If a competitor's company has just announced a price increase, it may give you hope they will raise price, but once again, you will assess their past behaviors after a price increase announcement. If they did not always follow through with their increases, you will be skeptical and less likely to increase your own price.

- If your competitor is unpredictable, mostly pricing high but occasionally using price to gain share (possible just from one rogue salesperson), you are much more likely to worry that this might be one of those occasions where they will drop again. Thus, you are likely to drop your own price in a preemptive move.

Of course, this goes both ways. Just as you think about this in assessing your competitor, so too are they assessing you in just the same way. What I often see is when a sales-person, believing the competitor might drop price, decides to drop price. This person believes they are doing this in response to the competitor. The competitor does not inter-pret this action as a response to their behavior. Instead, the competitor interprets that you are the aggressive one, using price to gain share. Now both parties begin to drop price. Both think they are doing it defensively and that the other started it!

When working with companies which have tough pric-ing markets, I often ask, *"Who is the player that is disruptive with price or pricing for share gain?"* Clients always point to one or more of their competitors. They never indicate they play a role in this negative pricing dynamic. Then I ask, *"If I were to ask your competitors who they thought was the price aggressive player in the market, how would they respond?"* At this point, many begin to see that their own behaviors might be viewed as price aggressive by competitors. They begin to take some ownership in the negative market dynamic. Recall the Simon-Kucher study I mentioned—of companies indicating they were in a price war, 88% of the respondents believed the other company started it! No doubt, many of these respondents failed to realize how their own behaviors contributed to the price war.

Picture this: You go into a negotiation with a strong belief that your competitor will hold or raise price. You are confident they will not use price to gain share. Just as they are confident that you will not use price to take their share. Your price decision is now about asking for your appropriate fair value. Life is good. Profits are up. Price negotiations are easy. *Sound like a dream world? Too good to be true?* Maybe so, but you can get close. You will never know with full certainty what your competition will do, but you can greatly increase the odds that they will be disciplined (i.e., not use low price to buy share) by adjusting your own behaviors. In training sessions, I always include a competition game so the participants experience the cause and effect of their actions—those that encourage higher prices and those that destroy market price. The results are so insightful and have real world application that I believe the exercise is worth sharing.

The Competition Game: One team plays against another team through many rounds of negotiations with the aim of maximizing their profits. For each negotiation, they decide on their price strategy—either increase price to gain profit or drop price to gain share. Four types of players consistently emerge, each with predictable profit results:

- **The Share Gain Players:** Time and time again, these players will drop price to gain share. Initially, they may get lucky and increase share if their competitor is taking a strategy of raising price. However, it doesn't take long for the competitor who is losing share to begin dropping price in a defensive move. By the end of the game, both competitors have low or even negative profits. In companies which have a strong 'volume-oriented' culture, I see many of these type players. Surprisingly, many of them stick to their 'drop price to gain share strategy' even as they watch their profits turn negative. They don't know any other way to do business.

- **The Clueless Players:** These players tend to act with no consistent, predictable strategy. In fact, their behaviors seem to be unrelated to the competitor's behaviors. At times they raise price and at times they drop price. There is no discernable pattern. Thus, their competitor is confused—feeling distrust they assume the worse (i.e., another price drop)—which leads to them dropping price with each negotiation. The result of this unpredictable behavior is low market price and low profits for both teams.

- **The Price Increaser:** These players have the best intentions. They fully understand that if both parties are disciplined (i.e., continue to go for higher price), both will achieve the highest profits. Unfortunately, when these players are faced with an aggressive competitor, they don't know what to do. They seemingly ignore the aggressive competitor, negotiation after negotiation, as their share continues to decline. Possibly they hope that the competitor will make an assumption that they are disciplined and will eventually follow their lead. *But why should the competitor do this?* Their strategy of dropping price and gaining share continues to work for them. They are not going to change this behavior until they experience a negative consequence. The Price Increasers have only learned half of the equation to optimize profits—the offensive skills. They know the value of a disciplined approach, but they have yet to learn the importance of reacting in a smart and purposeful way towards aggressive competitors (i.e., causing some negative consequence to the competitor). They need to learn defensive skills.

- **The Smart Player:** These players understand the value of disciplined pricing. They understand how their behaviors affect competitors and they actively work to encourage a disciplined marketplace. Their primary strategy is to raise price; however, they won't stand around and let competitors take their share without reacting. They retaliate in a thoughtful way so as not to start price wars. This team comes out with the most profit, and the collective profits of both competitors (i.e., the industry profitability) is the highest of all four types of players. These are the players that win the game.

This game is remarkably similar to real world pricing. These dynamics and results play out the same way time and time again in B2B markets.

Case Study 1.1:

A DuPont business acquired a competitor. This competitor had occasionally priced significantly below us. We had assumed their behavior was irrational. Yet, after the acquisition we found extensive documentation in their files of DuPont dropping prices as their rationale for their significant price drops. Our behavior had created their price aggression.

Force 2: The Customer Force

Just as your behaviors influence the behaviors of your competitors, they also influence the behaviors of your customers—perhaps even more so.

As a customer, would you rather buy tickets to a professional football game from an official box office or from a ticket scalper on the street? Most people choose the official box office. The primary reason is trust. People feel they can trust the official ticket counter to give them a fair price and a valid ticket. They know there are times when buying from a scalper might be cheaper, but in most cases they are unwilling to accept the risk. With the scalper, there is always the risk that the ticket price will be higher than the official box office price or that the ticket will not be valid. Clearly, trust and fairness dominate this buying decision and it trumps price more times than not.

The lesson here is the more your customers feel they are being fairly treated and the more they trust you, the more they will buy from you at a fair, yet higher price. Unfortunately, salespeople (perhaps influenced by their leaders' behaviors) often unintentionally display behaviors that create distrust in the customer's eyes.

Just the simple act of dropping price when customers push back on your price can create distrust. The customer is left wondering *if they had pushed back harder, would the price be even lower? Are other customers getting even better prices because they pushed back harder? Have they been paying too much all along?* Your price discounting action causes the customer to get even more price aggressive in the future.

Let's flip my original question from, "*Would you rather buy from an official ticket counter or a ticket scalper?*" to "*Would you rather compete with an official ticket counter or a ticket scalper?*" Once again, the answer I hear far more often is people would prefer to compete with an official ticket counter. Again, the primary reason comes back to trust. The perception is the official ticket counter will be fair, consistent, and predictable in their pricing. This in turn allows you to be more confident in pushing for your fair price. Yet, there are always a handful of folks who would rather compete against the ticket scalper. Once again, their rationale goes back to trust. They recognize they can win most customers because they are viewed as more trustworthy and fair than scalpers. I'm sure you are noticing a theme here. The backbone of good pricing behaviors starts with generating trust and fairness in the marketplace—in the eyes of customers, competitors, and even in the eyes of your own sales team.

By the way, the official ticket booth represents strategic competitors while the scalper represents non-strategic competitors. Non-strategic competitors might include new businesses that seem to pop up overnight or new low-priced, internet-based businesses. Many of these are here today and gone tomorrow. They never gain the customer's trust or they lose it based on performance. They must underprice strategic suppliers as their relative value to the customer is significantly less. Don't overreact with price drops to these non-strategic players.

Force 3: Your Behaviors

Do your own behaviors affect your colleagues' behaviors? You bet! Let's say you decide to give a large discount to a specific customer. You start out believing this is an unusual case that calls for a larger than normal discount. It's a hard decision and not easy to convince your manager, but eventually you both agree to the discount. The next time a difficult negotiation arises, it is even easier to decide to go with a large discount. *In fact, your peers have gotten wind of this large discount and they begin to ask for larger discounts too; after all, if you used it to gain volume, why shouldn't they?*

Leadership behaviors certainly affect the sales force behaviors. Having a business strategy to sell out assets or go for aggressive share gain in a mature market, or leadership being unwilling to risk volume are certain to drive behaviors that result in lower price and profits. Sales will default to dropping price. Buyers will sense this fear of losing volume, or desperation to gain volume, and will aggressively push on price.

Here are additional internal behaviors (fumbles)—often leadership driven—that create an atmosphere of less trust, less fairness, and more aggressive pricing:

- Sales incentives that are predominantly based on volume gain

- Leaders always asking about or celebrating volume/ share gains and neglecting to ask about or celebrate price gains

- Leaders asking sales to increase volume at the end of each quarter or year to meet business quarterly targets

- Setting floor prices for sales rather than, or in addition to, target prices (This behavior typically results in over 70% of deals falling to the floor price)

- The business (marketing managers or product managers) not ensuring the sales organization has the proper training on your offering's value proposition nor the appropriate sales collateral to effectively sell this value to their customers.

- Leaders taking customer calls during price increases and providing price relief the salesperson was unwilling to provide.

Not only do these behaviors create more price-aggressive pressures with your own sales force, but they also have unintended consequences. They lead towards more aggressive behaviors in your competitors and in your customers. The downward pricing spiral picks up speed.

Force 4: The Market Dynamic Force

You may have limited or no ability to influence large market dynamics such as recessions, oil price swings, or raw material price swings, but how you react to these changing dynamics can have a significant impact on market pricing. *When market dynamics turn favorable, are you quick to proactively take action and push for higher prices or are you conservative in your actions, inadvertently slowing the potential rise of the market price? Conversely, when market conditions turn unfavorable, do you drop price quickly or too deeply out of fear you might lose share? Or do you set deliberate strategies that stop or slow the decline of your price and the market price?* We will go into this topic in more detail in Plays 2 and 3, but recognize the way a sales force handles major market dynamic swings should be guided by the people who set your pricing strategy (not by each individual salesperson setting individual strategies). These leaders need to quickly and proactively assess the market and set strategies that will guide the sales teams. Then the sales team needs to act in concert.

The Dangers of Excessive Discounting

When I examine the discounting performance of a business, I quickly get a sense of how they are affecting the four market forces. Price/volume scatter plots, of virtually every business I work with (see Figure 1.2), show large scatter of prices for different customers buying the same product. On one hand, some variance is expected; we often must discount in the B2B world especially with large volume accounts or customers in lower value market/customer segments. On the other hand, when the price spread is large among customers of equal size, it raises a red flag. Most businesses discount far too frequently and far too deeply. When I see this, I know there are sales or leadership behaviors that are creating more aggressive competitors, more aggressive customers, and a more aggressive salesforce within their own business.

Figure 1.2. Price Scatter Plot

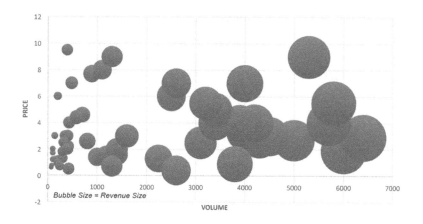

Let's consider customers first. We often tell ourselves that our pricing to any given customer is confidential. Other customers will never know we are discounting more to some customers. In today's world, that can be a costly mistake. It is becoming increasingly common for key people from one company to be lured away to a competing company or for one customer to buy out another customer's business. When customers are global, yet sales folks sell regionally, a salesperson in one region might offer a higher price than a salesperson in another region. When these things happen and your high priced customer finds out that others have lower prices, you can quickly lose trust with that customer or lose that customer completely. Oftentimes, the customer will push you harder for lower prices going forward, if they even remain with you.

Additionally, customers who were successful in getting low price are convinced it was their tough negotiation skills that led to this success–thus they will continue, if not ramp up, their tough negotiations.

Case Study 1:2

For years I have vacationed at a health and fitness spa in Mexico. I absolutely loved this week away from the office. I'd spend six to seven hours a day hiking, weightlifting, or doing yoga in a beautiful setting rather than sitting eight hours at my desk. I generally booked months, if not a full year, in advance. After many visits, I was talking with some guests who mentioned they had just decided to go to the resort at the last minute due to the great price discount they were offered. I went from relaxed and stress-free to steamed. Here I was, one of their loyal customers, and they were offering others lower prices.

The next year I decided to employ professional buyer tactics. I called the resort and told them I would only come if they offered me a discount. To my surprise, they quickly agreed. Over the next several years, I continued to call and ask for special discounts—always suggesting that I would not come without it or telling them I would bring a friend if they offered me a discount. If it didn't work, I politely asked for the manager. I played up the fact I was a very loyal customer, and I continued to suggest not coming or the lost opportunity of me not bringing along other guests. For years this strategy worked. I got discounts. Now you should know with each and every negotiation, I was bluffing. I fully intended to go, and if I discussed bringing another guest, I fully intended to bring that person along with or without the discount. Eventually, the resort got wise to their own poor pricing behaviors (or more likely recognized their true value). They stopped discounting. I used all my tricks to try getting the discount but to no avail. Was I upset? Oddly, no. In some ways, I was relieved. I now felt I could trust that the pricing to all guests was fair. I stopped asking for discounts, and I continue to go on vacations there once or twice a year. I had always felt that the price for this vacation was more than fair given the value they created. In fact, I would have gladly paid more. It was the fact that they were not treating me fairly, versus other guests, that created my mistrust. So much for my relaxing vacation!

Case Study 1.3:

On a professional side, one of the many DuPont businesses I coached had a very large customer with a substantial discount—a discount far larger than the few other customers of comparable size. This customer was adept at using (if not abusing) their pricing power. They insisted they would not pay for services, yet they continued to use more services than any other customer—a red flag that they did indeed value the services. Additionally, it was unlikely that another supplier could easily pick up this large volume and service them in the way they were accustomed. Driven by fear of losing this large customer, leadership was unwilling to follow my price increase recommendation. As happens more frequently than you might think, another large loyal buyer paying higher price found out about the lower price to this customer. As you might imagine, this buyer was furious and wasted no time letting DuPont know. This DuPont business was now in damage control. One of their largest most profitable buyers no longer trusted them. This customer threatened to shift share away. In the end, DuPont acquiesced to a significant price reduction to mitigate this situation. It took a long time before we regained *this buyer's trust—leading to years of working with a much more price aggressive customer.*

Let's turn to the impact on competitors from excessive discounting. Clearly competitors don't have access to your actual prices and scatter plots, however I contend your competitors form a mental model of what your prices might look like, and their mental model has them believing your prices are consistently lower than they actually are. The shaded area in Figure 1.3 shows how competitors might envision your scatter plot. This distorted view is a result of two factors:

- Your accounts with high prices are likely loyal to you and may even be sole sourced with you. Rarely are there bidding wars over this loyal business.

- Your lower-priced accounts are quite likely price-sensitive customers—customers who intentionally shop around and play one competitor off another competitor. These buyers never tell you when other suppliers have offered higher-priced products, but they are fast to let you know when they have lower-priced competitive offerings. In fact, such buyers will slant every piece of information they have to make you think you are higher priced than your competition.

Once again, your competitors mostly experience your pricing on the low-priced, competitive accounts. Of course, this works both ways. Oftentimes salespeople have a distorted view of the competitors' pricing—believing the competitors are consistently lower than they actually are. In either case, just a few low-priced bids, won or lost, contributes to an increase in price aggression.

Figure 1.3. Price Scatter Plot as Perceived by Competition

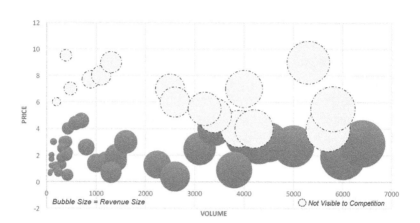

Case Study 1.4:

At DuPont, many of our businesses competed against another large chemical company. Time and again, our businesses would tell me that this large chemical company was disrupting the market with their low prices. Years later as a consultant, I had the opportunity to work with several businesses in this competitor's company. To my initial surprise, each of these businesses commented that DuPont had lower prices than they had. Both companies thought the other one was the lower-priced supplier. Clearly, only one of them can be right. Upon reflection, I realized that they both experienced each other's pricing in a small fraction of their accounts—the low-priced accounts.

Consistent with this belief, the Homburg study mentioned earlier found approximately 80% of companies believe their prices are higher than competition. Just 12% thought they are priced the same as competition while only 8% felt their prices are lower. As a chemical engineer, I know math and this story just doesn't add up. Likely only 10%–30% of the companies are higher, despite a full 80% thinking they are. The lesson (fumble) here is twofold: (1) You are likely mistaken if you think your price is consistently higher than your competition, and (2) Your competitors are likely more price aggressive because they mistakenly believe you frequently discount heavily.

Now that you know the typical fumbles, it's time to introduce the skills for winning the game.

Best Practice Behavior Guidelines for Pricing Execution

Pricing behavior best practice guidelines are anchored in creating trust and fairness in the marketplace. This influences the market price in a positive direction, legally and with integrity, ideally contributing a less aggressive market—a more disciplined market. There is no guarantee this will work since customers and competitors are free to act in any manner they see fit, but I have yet to see a business following these guidelines not be successful in shifting their marketplace towards less price aggression—often quite significantly.

Considering the flip side of this—creating distrust and unfairness within the marketplace—one can easily envision customers being skeptical of your price, thus, pushing hard for lower prices (maybe even shifting their volume elsewhere). You can envision competitors getting much more aggressive in their own pricing as a defensive move to your perceived attack. Clearly, this is not the way to be perceived. The bad news is, to some degree, many companies may already be perceived this way, though unintentionally.

THE MARKETPLACE DEFINED

The marketplace includes the following players:

- customers (i.e., their buyers, owners, leaders, influencers and users)

- competitors

- sales force

- downstream distributors and partners

- customer's customers

Being fair and trustworthy doesn't mean being a pushover or turning the other cheek. In fact, it is the opposite. It means having the confidence, the conviction, and the integrity to stand up for your fair price—to stand up to bullying tactics whether from customers pushing and threatening you for low price or competitors trying to intercept your share. Former professional basketball star Charles Barkley said it best: "*People always say turn the other cheek. If you turn the other cheek, I'm going to hit you in the other cheek too.*" It is imperative that you master both offensive and defensive skills.

Customers who are successful in pushing you for excessive discounts will only get more aggressive in pushing for discounts in the future. Competitors who successfully use price to take some of your share, with no negative consequences, will only get more aggressive in targeting your accounts. Stand up for your fair price with integrity and be sure you are not a price disruptor.

Figure 1.4 introduces the key offensive and defensive behaviors that you must master to create the trust and fairness that will lead to a less aggressive marketplace. Plays 2 and 3 will cover these skills in detail:

Figure 1.4. Disciplined Pricing Behavior Guidelines

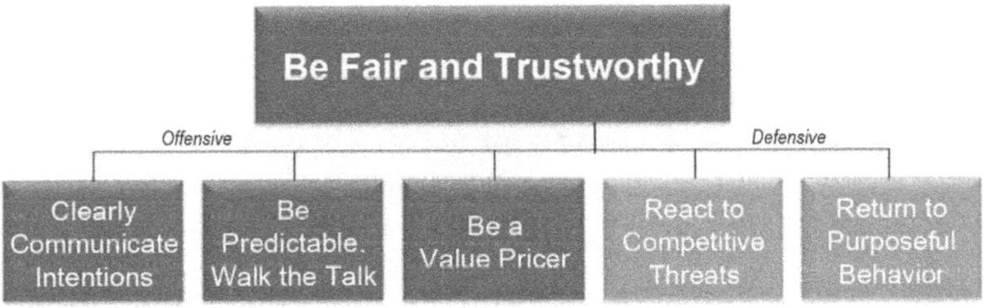

Offensives Moves:

- **Clearly Communicate Your Intentions:** Influencing your market starts with being clear about your intended actions. For price increases some level of transparency—not your specific prices just your increase percentage or amount—is needed to build trust, to build acceptance, and to be followed. Leaving your customers, partners, and competitors guessing about your actions creates distrust and misunderstanding which leads to greater price pressure. You need smart, visible communications of your price increase intentions (and potentially of other things like new products, new assets, etc.). Don't worry that competitors who know your game plan will use it against you. Your larger goal is to influence them to follow you—which can only be done if they know what you are doing and why. If they do follow you, you all win in a significant way. If they don't, and they are intent on using price to gain share, you are better positioned if they undercut your price increase rather than your current price.

- **Be Predictable—Walk the Talk:** Indicating your intentions is one thing, but if you fail to follow through you create more skepticism. You must be viewed by the marketplace as committing to your intentions. You must be predictable —predictable in the sense of doing what you say you will do. Unfortunately, too many companies are predictable in announcing a price increase and then backing down from the increase. This behavior creates enormous distrust. Even when not increasing price, predictability engenders trust.

- **Be a Value Pricer:** Pricing your offering with a premium for the value you deliver—whether in the product, the services, the brand/reputation, or the customer experience—is just one dimension of being a value pricer. The other dimension includes how you negotiate when a price discount (or backing off a price increase) needs to be considered. It is this negotiation behavior, if done poorly, that is likely the largest source in creating price-aggressive customers. A value pricer negotiates something in exchange for price concessions.

Defensive Moves:

- **React to Competitive Threats:** Reacting or retaliating towards a competitor's threat is part of good pricing. It is quite likely, at some point, to have a competitor target your accounts and try to 'buy' your share with excessive discounting. If you turn the other cheek, they will continue this behavior. They must feel a negative consequence to their behavior such as thoughtfully going after one of their accounts with low price.

- **Return to Purposeful Behavior:** Returning to purposeful behavior, after you have reacted to a competitive threat, is essential. Don't continue to aggressively go after this competitor's accounts with low prices. If you do, you will leave the competitor with no choice but to continue to price aggressively themselves. Before you know it, you have created a price war.

It may sound like I am suggesting you never attempt to gain share from your competitors. Of course not! Businesses need to continue to grow and doing so generally means taking volume from your competitors. I am, however, suggesting that taking share through offering excessive discounts is rarely a successful, sustainable model for profit growth. The side effects of destroyed profits (from lower price) and the likelihood of starting a price war resulting in even further profit loss are often too high. You are far better earning your share growth as discussed in Play 4. The rare cases when using price to 'buy" share might make sense are discussed in Play 3.

Now that you have the basics for influencing the marketplace, it's time to tackle price/volume trade-off decisions.

Chapter 2:
Price/Volume Trade-Off Decisions

Price/volume trade-off decisions are possibility one of the most misunderstood aspects of pricing—one of the biggest fumbles that salespeople (and often their business, marketing, and sales leaders) routinely make. Get your price too high and your volume is likely to suffer. Conversely, lower your price enough and you may gain volume, but your profits may suffer. From a strategic standpoint, business and sales leaders periodically consider price increases across their product lines and the potential risk of losing volume. Yet, sales professionals are making these decisions with every tough negotiation. *Can I get more price without losing volume? Would I be better off lowering my price to gain more share?* These decisions are *proactive* decisions. You are actively deciding whether you want to optimize volume or price.

Sales teams are also frequently faced with *reactive* price/volume decisions as well. Reactive decisions occur when there is a competitive threat and you must decide whether to respond by lowering your price to protect your volume. This chapter focuses on proactive trade-off decisions. Reactive trade-off decisions will be covered in Chapter 8.

Except for a few rare situations, price/volume decisions should be done so you optimize your company's earnings. Healthy profits are essential for companies to stay in business as well as to continue to fund the sales team, services, and innovation. For sales teams that are compensated on volume alone, the odds are extremely high that profit-destroying decisions are being made daily.

Price/volume trade-off decisions can get a bit technical and mathematical. To make this more palatable, this section is broken into two parts. Part 1 focuses on the least amount of 'technical, mathematical' information you need for practical, actionable, and smart pricing decisions. Part 2 goes into more theory on these decisions.

PROACTIVE PRICE/VOLUME TRADE-OFF DECISION DEFINED

A proactive decision is one made when deciding your strategy to go for higher price and risk volume or to lower price for volume gain. It excludes decisions that are in response (reactive) to competitive moves. The price/volume trade-off calculation determines the point where the change in price equals the change in volume from a profit standpoint; i.e., profits are neutral—the earnings are the same whether you have that volume change or that price change. For example, if you drop price by 10% and the price/volume break-even point is 50% then to recover your lost profits from the price drop you must gain 50% share. If you gain less volume than 50%, you will have lost profits. On the other hand, if you gain more than 50% share, you will have improved profits.

Part 1: A Practical View

Let's assume you have the choice of selecting one of the four goals listed below upon which your compensation will be based. The closer you come to hitting your goal the more you will be paid. Let's further assume that the product line you are selling is fairly undifferentiated yet your company has a strong position, brand, and reputation. Which goal would you like to be measured against?

1. *Price increase 10%:* with up to a 12% share loss allowed

2. *Price increase 5%:* no share loss allowed

3. *Volume gain 75%:* with up to a 10% price drop allowed

4. *Volume increase 17%:* with no price drop allowed

Almost everyone invariably selects number one or number two: price increase options. Intuitively savvy commercial folks understand that getting 5%–10% price increase is far more attainable than trying to get 17%–75% share gain. You know that your competition will not stand idly by and allow you to take substantial share away from them. They will retaliate with price drops of their own to defend, if not win back, their share.

However, did your intuition tell you that all four of the goals above would deliver equal profits? That's right, identical earnings! Few business leaders or sales professionals would naturally assume this relationship. In fact, most tend to 'unknowingly' operate on the assumption that a 10% price increase is relatively equal in profit value to a 10% volume gain. While that would be true if we were considering revenue, it is far off when we consider earnings. This is the reason why there are so many profit-destroying decisions relative to price and volume trade-offs. And, why it is so important to understand how to make smart price/volume trade-off decisions. The example I used above was based on the average Fortune 1000 company. The price/volume trade-off for your business and each of its products will be different; thus, the need for some math.

The Proactive Price/Volume Trade-Off Framework

This framework has four steps:

1. Get your contribution margin percent.
2. Calculate the price/volume trade-off break-even point.
3. Estimate your likely volume change.
4. Assess the market implications.

Step 1. Get your contribution margin percent: Contribution margin is the margin that results when variable production costs are subtracted from revenue. Businesses' contribution margin percentages can vary widely from 0%–100%, but here are some generalities that often hold true:

- Commodity product lines typically have a lower contribution margin than specialty product lines. While 10%–30% is not uncommon, better performing commodities may even be closer to 40% or higher when market conditions are favorable.

- Specialty or differentiated product lines are more likely to be in the 40%–65% range.

- Many businesses have a mix of both undifferentiated and differentiated products; thus, it is not uncommon to see average business margins in the 30%– 50% range. The average of the Fortune 1000 companies is in the ballpark of 30%.

- Distributors often, though not always, operate with lower contribution margins.

Your financial analyst or pricing resource should be able to give you the contribution margin for your largest product lines if you don't have direct access to this data. There is no need to be precise, but do get in the ballpark. If your product line has a margin of 32%, just think of it as approximately 30%. Ideally, if the data is available, and you are making a customer-specific decision, it is better to use the customer-specific contribution margin, especially if the customer has a much lower price than the average customer price. It is not unusual to see a low-priced customer have a contribution margin 10–20 percentage points below the average contribution margin.

CONTRIBUTION MARGIN PERCENT DEFINED

The *variable* contribution margin (CM) % is your revenue minus your variable or incremental costs (i.e., those costs such as raw material costs or freight costs that increase with each additional unit of sale) divided by your revenue. CM% = (revenue - incremental costs)/revenue

Step 2. Calculate the Price/Volume Trade-off Break-even Point: To calculate the volume break-even percentage, see Table 2.1. Note the left side of the table is for *price increase* break-even situations and the right half of the table is for price *decrease* situations. Using this table, let's assess a typical commodity product that has a contribution margin of 20%:

- *Price Increase 10%:* If you opt to increase your price 10%, the volume break-even point is 33%. You could afford to lose as much as 33% share without hurting your profits! If you lose less than 33% share, your profits will increase.

- *Price Drop 10%:* If you opt to drop price 10%, the volume break-even point is 100%. You would need to gain more than 100% share (double your volume!) just to break-even on earnings. Any volume share gain less than that would be destroying profits.

⚒ Table 2.1. Proactive Price/Volume Break-Even Table

Proactive Break-Even Volume for Price Change Look Up Table								
BREAK-EVEN VOLUME FOR VOLUME CHANGE	**Break-Even Volume** *Volume You Can Afford to Lose & Hold Profits*				**Break-Even Volume** *Volume You Must Gain to Hold Profit*			
	Price Increase Action				**Price Decrease Action**			
Contribution Margin	2%	5%	10%	20%	-2%	-5%	-10%	-20%
10%	17%	33%	50%	67%	25%	100%		
15%	12%	25%	40%	57%	15%	50%	200%	
20%	9%	20%	33%	50%	11%	33%	100%	
25%	7%	17%	29%	44%	9%	25%	67%	400%
30%	6%	14%	25%	40%	7%	20%	50%	200%
35%	5%	13%	22%	36%	6%	17%	40%	133%
40%	5%	11%	20%	33%	5%	14%	33%	100%
45%	4%	10%	18%	31%	5%	13%	29%	80%
50%	4%	9%	17%	29%	4%	11%	25%	67%
55%	4%	8%	15%	27%	4%	10%	22%	57%
60%	3%	8%	14%	25%	3%	9%	20%	50%
65%	3%	7%	13%	24%	3%	8%	18%	44%
70%	3%	7%	13%	22%	3%	8%	17%	40%
75%	3%	6%	12%	21%	3%	7%	15%	36%

Proactive Break-Even Calculations Assuming Zero Opportunity Cost

As you can see, in low contribution margin product lines (typically undifferentiated products), price is a far more powerful lever than volume in generating profits. Many business leaders of commodity products mistakenly believe they must drop price to keep their plants running full out—they think that this is the key to being successful. This is a fumble and there are penalties to be paid. Low margin businesses are typically much more successful when they push for every price increase they can get and resist price drops—even if it means not running full out.

Using the break-even table, let's explore the price/volume trade-off for a specialty product line with a reasonably high margin of 50%:

- *Price Increase 10%:* If you opt to increase price 10%, the volume break-even point is 17%. You could afford to lose as much as 17% share without hurting your profits. If you lose less than 17% share, your profits will increase.

- *Price Drop 10%:* If you opt to drop price 10%, the volume break-even point is 25%. You would need to gain more than 25% share just to break-even on earnings. Any volume gains less than that would be destroying profits.

The pricing lever for higher margin products is still far more powerful than the volume lever at generating profits, but it is not nearly as dramatic as seen for undifferentiated products with low margins.

The bottom line is that price, for nearly all businesses, is a more powerful lever to gain profits than the volume lever. On average (for the Fortune 1000 companies), the price lever is four to five times as powerful as the volume lever. A 4% gain in share would be needed to equal the earnings impact of a 1% gain in price. Likewise, a 1% drop in price would need roughly a 5% gain in volume for equal earnings.

PRICE/VOLUME TRADE-OFF TIP

Use this 'rule of thumb' for price drop to volume gain trade-offs for your top one to three product lines.

- 1% Price Drop = 10% Volume Gain (for a 20% contribution margin product)

- 1% Price Drop = 5% Volume Gain (for a 30% contribution margin product)

- 1% Price Drop = 3.3% Volume Gain (for a 40% contribution margin product)

- 1% Price Drop = 2.5% Volume Gain (for a 50% contribution margin product)

Caution: Occasionally check your product line contribution margin. If your business has experienced a large raw material cost change or your price has changed, your contribution margin can significantly change.

Step 3. Estimate Your Likely Volume Change: Predict—to the best of your ability—what is likely to happen to your volume when you change price. Then, compare this expectation to the break-even volume.

- *If you are planning a price increase, how much volume are you realistically likely to lose?* If it is less than the break-even volume, you will probably proceed with the price increase.

- *If you drop price, how much volume are you realistically likely to gain?* If it is less than the break-even volume, you should probably avoid dropping the price.

Step 4. Assess the Market Implications: There are market implications to any price change. You are not raising price or dropping price in a vacuum. There will be competitive moves and customer moves you must also consider.

Implications of Dropping Price: Consider the risks listed below. In my experience, many of these are likely to occur making any price-drop strategy a potentially losing strategy:

- Competitor(s) drops price as well to defend their share.

- Your customer believes pushing for lower price works and they get more aggressive in the future.

- Your price drop spreads to other markets or accounts that you had not intended.

- Other sales representatives on your team see your action and it encourages them to drop price more often.

- The customer never had any real intention of buying from you. They just wanted your low price offer to leverage their current supplier. The current supplier, forced to lower their price to retain the account, now becomes more price aggressive in the market.

- Your actions contribute to mistrust in the marketplace, creating a more aggressive marketplace with a lower market price.

The potential volume gain you hope to achieve with a price drop had better be substantial because you are taking a large risk. If you do decide to proceed, be sure to use some of the techniques discussed in Play 3 to minimize risks.

Implications of a Price Increase: The potential negative implications of a price increase are fewer:

- You lose much more volume than anticipated, especially if competitors don't follow your price increase.

- You don't lose much volume today (e.g., perhaps customers are locked-in short term) but you lose volume in the future.

The approaches discussed in Chapter 5 will go a long way to not only mitigating these price increase risks but potentially fully off-setting them.

Skill Drill:

Your Challenge: Your sales force believes they can grow sales by 20% if the business will agree to drop the price by 10%. *Should you do this?* Presume the contribution margin of this business is 50%.

Analysis: First look up the price/volume trade-off break-even point for a 10% price drop using break-even Table 2.1. Hopefully you identified the break-even volume as 25%. You need to gain 25% more volume just to break-even. You will need far more than 25% gain to increase your profits sufficiently to offset the many potential negative risks. Sales has estimated only a 20% volume gain. You should not do this price drop; it will result in lower profits for the business.

Part 2: The Math

This section describes price/volume trade-off decisions for those interested in more detail and theory.

The Break-even % Volume Change

The actual break-even calculation used to generate Table 2.1 is:

Break-even % Volume Change = (-% Change in Price)/ (% Contribution Margin – % Change in Price).

This equation holds true for all cases except when you are sold out or nearly sold out. In those cases, you also need to consider opportunity costs.

Opportunity costs are actually the potential profits you may be passing up to make this deal. In other words, if you fill up your assets with low price business then along comes a customer willing to pay a higher price, you have no product to sell them. Essentially, you have lost the opportunity to go after higher-priced business. A simple way to think about the price/volume trade-off when you are sold out or nearly so is: never drop your price, in fact, increase your price. *Why?* Because the risk is low. If the industry is also tight, the customer may not be able to find an alternative source, and if they do it is likely to be high priced. Even if you lose the account, in a tight market you are likely to be able to place this volume at a higher price elsewhere.

Contribution Margin versus Full Margin

The break-even table (Table 2.1) and the equation above are both based upon *variable* contribution margin; they essentially ignore fixed costs (e.g., people costs, maintenance costs, etc.). The equation presumes a short-term (not multiyear) price/volume decision. Over the short term, fixed cost can't be changed—that's why they are called fixed! So, whether your price or your volume goes up or down, these fixed costs remain essentially unchanged. For example, rarely would you shut down a manufacturing asset (laying off your operators and mechanics as well as mothballing or tearing down the asset) or lay off a large portion of your leadership, research, or commercial resources without considerable time to prepare. Thus, for the short term, we can assume the fixed costs are the same before and after the price or volume change. This assumption allows us to leave it out of the equation.

If it is a long-term or a multiyear strategy, then you must consider fixed cost. Be sure your pricing is high enough to cover your full cost. If this is not occurring, then your business leadership has larger, more strategic decisions to consider such as exiting this business, restructuring assets/resources, or raising price despite volume risks as a first step towards repairing or exiting the business.

Case Study 2.1:

In an earlier role at DuPont, I took responsibility for a commodity-based product that was in a slowly declining market. The assets, which historically ran at high utilization, were no longer fully sold out but the average contribution margin was good. As I examined the business, I realized we had many customers with excessive discounts and low contribution margins. In turned out that most of these were new accounts that the sales leader was targeting using lower price. The sales leader mistakenly assumed that given our excess capacity, as long as we covered our variable costs, we were making more money for the business. What he failed to realize was our behavior was hurting the industry from achieving higher prices and the incremental profit he generated was not enough to cover the full costs of our highest-cost plant.

I elected to close our highest-cost plant, at a fixed-cost savings of $5 million/year, which forced us to shed accounts. We opted to significantly raise our prices to encourage low-priced customers to leave. We were so successful with the price increase, that even with lower volume, our profits increased further. As we changed our behaviors, competitors started to increase their price as well. This gave us the confidence to increase yet again leaving us with far more profits, despite selling less volume and closing a manufacturing operation.

Case Study 2.2:

During the 2009 recession, many B2B industries were suffering with 30%–40% demand declines. Within DuPont, as in many other companies, a number of businesses decided to permanently shut down their older, high-cost assets. As they came out of the recession and demand began to grow, they had less capacity and were thus more price focused. Roughly three quarters of these businesses ended up with higher earnings despite having reduced capacity (thus reduced sales). It was clear that their past inadvertent decision to sell out assets had been hurting their price and the market price.

These fundamentals are the backbone of your pricing game whether you are increasing price or faced with having to drop price. We will build on these skills in Play 2 and Play 3.

Play 1:
Skill Drills to Build Your Game Plan

1. Which competitors in your industry, including yourselves, are the most price aggressive—pricing for share gain? How would your competitors answer this same question?

2. List the behaviors that you, or your business, do which potentially encourage a higher market price or create less aggressive customers and competitors.

3. List the behaviors that you, or your business, do which potentially hurt the market price or create more aggressive customers and competitors.

4. Obtain the (variable) contribution margin for your top one to three products. Using Table 2.1, determine:
   a. How much volume you must gain to offset a 10% drop in price for each product?
   b. How much volume you could afford to lose if you raised your price 10% for each product?

5. What actions or behaviors will you, or your business, do differently going forward?

PLAY 2:
THE SKILLS FOR FAIR PRICE AND PRICE-INCREASE NEGOTIATIONS

In football terms, this section is about offensive plays and special plays. You are not just going for a touchdown; you are going for a big win. You want to manage the field as well as your own tactical performance. You want to be sure you raise your price to its fair competitive position, yet you also want to proactively put upward pressure on the market price—a win-win. You are going to use your full pricing power and use it with confidence. Winning football teams consistently exhibit this bolder approach with skill.

Special plays relate to value pricing—getting a fair premium over competition when you deliver additional value. If your company has invested in creating extra value, it is only fair that you get fairly compensated for this value. Businesses with differentiated or specialty products generally understand this concept, although they often fail to use best practices that would enable them to get their highest appropriate price. On the other hand, businesses with undifferentiated or commodity products often ignore value pricing completely. This is a fumble. Undifferentiated products frequently have value in their services, reliability, consistent quality, brand, or customer experience that deserves a price premium.

Skilled value pricing goes beyond just capturing your fair price premium. Done well, or even done at a mediocre level, it creates trust with the customer. It defuses the price aggressive buyer. Done poorly, it creates distrust and price aggressive buyers as well as encourages the customer to begin evaluating other suppliers. As other suppliers get in the game, the price pressure ramps up even further.

One of the biggest impacts on your profitability is the market price. The good news is your behaviors can influence this price. The bad news is that if you are not proactively managing your behaviors, they are likely negatively impacting the market price. Successful increases will require you to master offensive best practices. The football analogy would be when the offensive team is on the 4th down with one yard to go and rather than take the traditional conservative play of punting, they have the courage and skill to go for it on the 4th down. Leadership, product management, and marketing will need to step up their game to give sales a winning shot.

While large businesses potentially affect the market price more than medium-sized businesses—especially if the market is not too fragmented—even relatively small companies can have a negative effect. Certainly, all suppliers' behaviors—even small companies in fragmented markets—influence the price aggressiveness of their own customers.

Let's tackle value pricing first.

Chapter 3:
Value Pricing for Specialty and Commodity Businesses

Outperforming your competition by delivering greater benefits to your customers is key to getting premium prices and growth. Unfortunately, far too many companies price below their fair price point. *Value pricing or value-in-use pricing,* as it is sometimes called, refers to an understanding—financially quantified where possible—of your value and your customer's willingness to pay a fair price for this value. In other words, they are willing to pay you a premium over competitors who offer less value. Here are the biggest fumbles I see relative to value pricing:

- Believing only specialty product lines need to use these concepts; they are not useful in commodity or undifferentiated product lines

- Believing value deserving a price premium is only created in the product features, and price premiums can't be charged for services, the customer experience, or your brand/reputation

- Not understanding or quantifying your own value and/or not being able to effectively convince your customers of this value

- Providing the same high value offering to customers who indicate they don't need extra value and won't pay a premium as to those who are willing to pay a premium

Value may come from a variety of elements:

- *Specialty Products:*
  - Product features

- *Commodity and Specialty Products:*
  - Product quality
  - Services: technical service, application development, auditing, training, analysis, certifications, special packaging, special quality assurances, etc.
  - Customer experience beyond services: reliability, security of supply, ease of doing business, responsiveness, providing valuable insights, good communications, excellent salespeople, or excellent customer service representatives, etc.
  - Brand and reputation

Any of the above features may allow you to get a price premium if the customer believes the value is real and is confident of their ability to fully tap into this value.

Specialty Products

There is emerging eye-opening data from LeveragePoint that indicates companies that use best practice value-pricing tools and techniques achieve between 5%–25% higher price premiums and a 5%–15% higher close rates than those who do not.[4] Creating value will result in higher price and higher volume if you use these best practice skills to capture it.

Specialty products generally have their largest benefits in their product features. If you have thousands of products, it is not practical to delineate the benefits for all products. Encourage your business to, at a minimum, complete value quantification along with value-selling collateral on your largest and/or most differentiated products. Value calculators or other value-based tools can help sales easily customize the value for each of their customers.

Commodity Products

I have worked with commodity products that have a 5%, 10%, and even 20% price premium in some of their market segments due to the added value the supplier creates beyond the product. For undifferentiated products, beyond quality, the benefits are all in the non-product features. The good news is that these features are typically the same across all your products; you can quantify the value once and apply this premium to all your products.

Case Study 3.1:

A distributor in the food service industry sold to a reseller who split their purchases among three suppliers. The industry was commoditized and very competitive. This distributor proactively worked with the end user (the reseller's customer) to sell the value of a branded container (i.e., the end user's logo placed on the container). The end user was delighted with this option and willing to pay a higher price. Since this was a branded product, the reseller had to buy 100% through this distributor. The distributor ended up with higher volume and higher price. The reseller had higher margin and the end user was delighted.

Customer Confidence in the Value

The closer customers are to having 100% confidence that your offering will deliver the stated value, the more likely you are to get a higher premium. As their confidence drops, they mentally (and often subconsciously) discount the value of your offering in their minds; thus, their willingness to pay extra decreases. The most effective ways to convince customers of your value are through one or more of the following:

- Quantifying the value from the customer's viewpoint

- Performing trials in the customer's operations

- Providing testimonials, endorsements, and/or case studies from other customers, especially those that are well respected in their industry

- Receiving third party endorsements (e.g., Voted best…, Awarded…, Certified by…,)

- Offering money back guarantees or warranties

Quantifying the value, in financial terms, tops the lists in getting your highest price. Not only are you likely to convince yourself that your business deserves a higher price than you originally thought, but you are also equipped to convince your customers to pay this appropriate price premium.

Quantifying Your Value

Which of these consultant's value propositions would you find both more compelling and be willing to pay more for if you were hiring a pricing expert to conduct a pricing course for your sales team?

> **Consultant 1:** I have trained sales teams in hundreds of businesses. We offer one day to three-day options.

> **Consultant 2:** I have trained sales teams in hundreds of businesses from single day to multi-day workshops. Course options include practical approaches and tools that both increase the confidence of the

sales team and allow them to immediately begin using the newly acquired knowledge for smarter price decisions. Multi-day workshops include developing specific business pricing plans which have resulted in many businesses achieving annualized price improvements of 1%—3% (e.g., $10 - $30 million profits on a $1 billion business).

Client endorsements affirm the course value:

"I was delighted with the strategy workshop & course. She led and pushed us to new promising strategies. I would highly recommend this approach to other businesses." ~SVP of Marketing & Sales

"This pricing course was fantastic. She provided practical insights and is a great teacher who knows her stuff. I would recommend this course." ~Director of Global Sales

"This is the best course I have taken in my career. Our full sales force should take this course." ~European Sales Manager

Which consultant's value proposition would you choose? Hopefully you selected Consultant 2 (and if you are wondering, the results and endorsements are real and the consultant is me). *Why?* Because you get a sense of the unique features of the offering and the financial impact stated in the customer's terms. As in most training courses, it can be difficult to quantify the full value, so I use endorsements and case study results from my other clients to affirm the value.

Let's look at a product-oriented example. *Which of these two examples are more compelling to both close the deal and do it at a higher price?*

Argument 1: Our product has the best heat resistance in the industry.

Argument 2: Our product has the best heat resistance in the industry. The higher heat resistance will improve your operation's yield by 10%, thus lowering your costs by 10%. This will save you $20,000 in costs or the equivalent of $0.2/lb.

Argument 1 leaves it to the customer to figure out why higher heat resistance is a good thing, what it will do for them, and how much that is worth financially. Many buyers wouldn't be able to make these leaps even if they had the time and inclination. Thus, the second argument is preferable.

⚒ *Value Proposition*: The most compelling arguments contain four elements:

1. *Feature:* Your offering feature(s) that make it unique—relative to the customer's alternative option

2. *Feature Benefit:* The benefit(s) this feature brings to the customer versus the alternative—quantified if possible

3. *Value Driver:* How the benefits bring financial value to the customer (i.e., lower cost, higher revenue or lower working capital)

4. *Financial Benefit:* Quantified financial benefit to the customer

Figure 3.1 demonstrates the best practice *economic value estimation (EVE)* approach to quantifying as well as illustrating your value to customers. Preparing an EVE is typically done with a cross-functional team (i.e., marketing, product management, pricing, sales and technical) led by marketing or pricing.

Start by identifying the customer's next best alternative option(s). The option of buying from another competitor—

either an in-kind product (e.g., plastic) or a not-in-kind product (e.g., wood or metal)—will result in your incremental value-add. The alternative option of the customer doing it themselves or doing nothing will result in your total or true value-add. It may strengthen your customer conversation to know the result of both your incremental value and your total value.

The group then hypothesizes offering features, potential benefits, value drivers, and the financial quantification to the customer. Identifying the benefits and value drivers for each feature are relatively easy (see Table 3.1 for examples). Estimating the actual amount (e.g., 10% yield improvement) and quantifying the value to the customer (e.g., $20,000 per year) is the challenging part. Yet the knowledge of a cross-functional group frequently leads to an acceptable solution. Your marketing or pricing resource may need to do some market validation and refinement on any hypotheses for which the group is less certain.

Figure 3.1. Economic Value Estimation

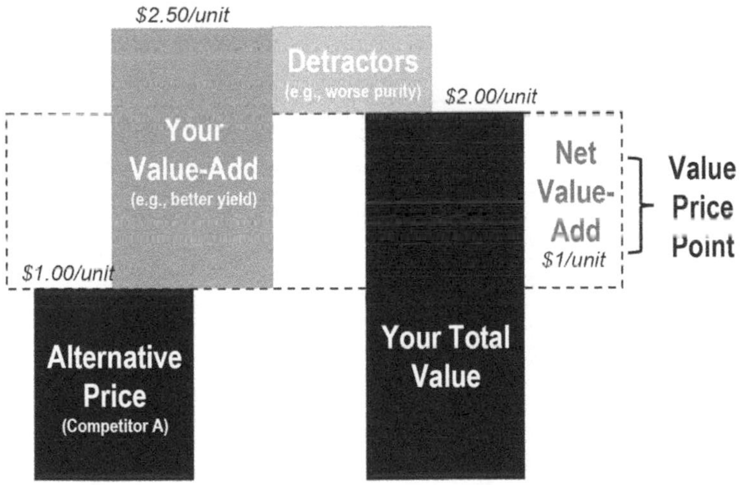

Table 3.1. Example Benefits and Value Drivers

Example Benefits	Drivers: Cost, Revenue or Capital
Improved Yield	Reduced Cost
Less Maintenance	Reduced Cost
Reduced Manpower	Reduced Cost
Reduced Energy	Reduced Cost
Improved Up-time	Reduced Cost or Higher Revenue
Better Product	Higher Revenue
Higher Follow On Sales	Higher Revenue
More Capacity	Higher Revenue or Reduced Capital
Less Equipment / Assets	Reduced Capital
Less Inventory	Reduced Working Capital
Longer Payment Terms	Reduced Working Capital

Sales must understand the concepts of value pricing in order to customize or refine the value (thus potentially the price) to each individual customer. In this example, if the customer were to tell you they believe a 10% yield is too high and 8% is the maximum improvement they can achieve, you could easily change the 10% to 8% in a value calculator to show the customer the revised financial results are $16,000 or $0.16/lb.

With the EVE complete, you know the extra value you create versus the customer's next best alternative. Your price should be set to share this value-add with your customer; you capture some of the value in price premiums and the customer enjoys the remaining value. As a default, you might split the value-add 50/50. In rare cases, the supplier might get a larger split, say 70%, when the benefits are certain, immediate, and there are few viable alternatives for the customer. More often, you may need to split 30%–40% of the value to you and 60%–70% to the customer. This might occur when the benefits to the customers are not perceived as certain, the return on their investment takes years to achieve (such as in a large equipment investment), or there is a big upfront cost for the customer to begin using your offering.

Your benefits will likely fall into three buckets:

- Financially quantifiable benefits such as yield improvement or reduced manpower

- Benefits which are often possible yet difficult to quantify such as reliability, short lead time, improved safety, or training

- Intangible benefits (sometimes referred to as soft benefits) such as societal value (e.g., greener products, a happier community) or emotional value (e.g., better relationships, improved brand/reputation, better appearance to the consumer)

The more you can financially quantify the benefits, the more likely you are to convince the customer that the benefits are certain; thus, your price premium will be higher. Realistically, this is not always possible. For features that are difficult to financially quantify, do your best to quantify the benefit improvement (e.g., 5%–10% yield improvement, or 1%–3% price improvement from training workshops) and identify the value driver even if you are unable to calculate the financial gain to the customer. Strengthen these arguments through case studies, endorsements, plant trials, or research findings, as with the training illustration shared earlier in this section. Here are a few additional examples using partially quantified data to communicate value:

- *Reliability:* Each year in your industry, there are typically two or three incidents of suppliers having unexpected outages and not being able to supply. The average supply issue lasts four days, costing the stocked-out customers on average four days of lost potential sales.

- *Safety:* Our product reduces 20%–40% of injuries. A work-related injury results in an average loss of approximately $38,000 including wages, productivity loss, and medical expenses per the National Safety Council (2005).

- ***Better Appearance:*** With comparable products having better appearance, customers have reported a 5%–10% improvement in revenue from increased price and/or volume.

When it comes to intangibles and benefits which are difficult to quantify, you still deserve a price premium, yet how much may be difficult to gauge. You probably have experienced sales leaders that can estimate a reasonable premium based on their experience. For many businesses, this might be in the 1%–5% range conservatively.

Since this book is focused on price execution for sales, I haven't gone into depth on value-in-use price setting. There are numerous good books that cover this topic. I have a section on it in my book *"The Pricing and Profit Playbook"* or consider *"The Strategies and Tactics of Pricing"* by Thomas Nagel and John Hogan.

Not all customers will value your products equally. As a result, you need to understand the different value segments and provide an appropriate value offering and value price per each segment.

Segmentation

Consider segments that may have different needs or value for your offering. If your product has extremely high purity, it may have very high value when you sell it into the electronics industry but no value to the automotive market who would be unwilling to pay any extra for higher purity. Consider these typical segments:

- market or application segments (e.g., cosmetics, electronics, automotive)

- regional segments (e.g., Europe, U.S., cities, rural areas)

- value-chain segments (e.g., direct customer, distributor, agent)

- Customer needs-based segments (e.g., price buyers, value buyers, relationship buyers)

It is relatively easy to identify your customers by market, region, and value chain position as well as to understand the varying needs of each of these segments. Additionally, if these segments don't interact or compete, you can often price them differently for the same product without risking a negative reaction from another segment.

Customer needs-based segmentation is the most difficult to manage, yet doing so is essential to making smart pricing decisions. These segments are harder to identify; they exist as a subset of each of the other segment types. For example, within any given market segment there is likely to be a group of customers that are focused almost totally on price. They are unwilling to pay extra for services, better quality, or higher performing products. Instead, they will shift to a lower-value supplier if they can get a lower price. Within this same market segment, there are other groups of customers that do value some of your features, perhaps your services or your higher performing products, and they are willing to pay a premium for this extra value. Chapter 6 is devoted to helping you understand and identify these segments as well as set pricing strategies and tactics for each segment.

The key issues to understand at this point are two-fold: First, if you want to maximize your *volume*, you will need to have a low-priced offering for your price-sensitive customers. Second, if you also want to maximize your *profits*, your low-priced offering must be of lesser value than your standard higher-priced offering. If a customer group is unwilling to pay for extra value, then their offering should be a lower value offering. The motto is: *"You get what you pay for."* That is how a value pricer operates. Neglecting to do this will undoubtedly foster mistrust and a more aggressive marketplace. Customers who are willing to pay a premium will not do so if other customers are getting the same offering at a lower price. Price-sensitive customers will be emboldened by their past success to push even harder for lower prices. This is one of the big hurdles to being a value pricer.

Equipment companies and specialty product lines often offer different brands or different products to serve the different markets or customer needs-based segments. An air conditioning manufacturer might supply the construction industry with a low-end air conditioner for their low-end housing, a mid-value brand for mid-range homes, and a high-value brand for the high-end homes. This is an excellent way to address different customer needs-based segments—it optimizes both price and volume.

Unfortunately, far too many companies who have invested in different brands, lose this advantage (i.e., they fumble) if their sales force is not disciplined enough to only sell the better brands to the customers willing to pay a fair price. I can't tell you how many times I have heard salespeople say, *"But the customer didn't want the low-end brand, so I had to give them the better brand at a reduced price. Their downstream customers want the better brand."*

This kind of thinking devalues the better brand and begins to make the low-end brand irrelevant. The salesperson should have realized that there must be value to this customer in the better brand or they would not have insisted on getting it. The value-in-use may well be downstream to your customer's customer. Yet it has the value to your direct customer of either increasing their sales or their price to their downstream customer. Furthermore, customers are likely insisting on the better brand, at low price, because it works; they request this each time and each time you concede. You may have created this monster, but you can tame it, too.

Case Study 3.2:

When I was starting up my price consulting firm, I went to LegalZoom® to form my legal entity (Limited Liability Corporation). Their website showed three offerings with three different price points. The basic offering was strictly the forming of the LLC at a low price. This was the offering I was interested in, after all, I didn't yet have any clients. I was clearly a price buyer. As I talked to the customer representative, she pointed out that their higher-end offering (at higher price) included many things that new business owners needed. She asked, "Don't you need a website? Marketing help? And ..."

Well, yes, I sure did need some of these items but certainly not all the items in this offering. I tried to convince her to give me a discount on their highest end offering by removing a few of the extra items that I did not need. I got nowhere. She insisted if I wanted elements of the highest-end offering, I had to buy the full offering at the full price. I was slightly disappointed but quite impressed with her integrity. I did buy the highest-end offering and felt I had been fairly treated. I continue to do business with them today.

Many companies do not have the advantage of having multiple brands; they may only have one product. Even so, they must act as a value pricer. They need to think in terms of the customer giving something of value to them or they need to take something away. If the customer wants to pay less, they get less or they give you something of value. Examples of *gives* might include getting more volume or a longer contract. On the *take* side, you might reduce their payment terms, lengthen their lead-time, or remove some services.

Internet Sales Channels

Many B2B companies are venturing into internet sales channels. This is done as an offensive move to either provide a low-priced sales option or to reach more potential customers. Web-based sales channels can be an excellent growth option, yet it comes with significant price risks. These suggestions will mitigate some of the risks:

- Consider not publicly sharing your price list. Have your existing customers sign into their specific account to view their specific pricing.

- If you publish your price list, avoid having these prices set lower (or significantly lower) than your traditional business. Doing this could risk traditional customers demanding these low prices. There is a proliferation of new web-based companies popping up—they have less value than established suppliers and must use low price to entice customers to try them. If you lower your price, these competitors will lower even further. As long as they can earn some profit, they will continue to undercut you. You are better to publish a higher price and have them undercut that, than to lower your prices and have them undercut these.

- Streamline your offering—strip it down so that you can reduce your internal costs as you reduce your price. Then be sure you diligently offer only this stripped-down version. Don't allow customers to talk you into giving them additional services or value that should be reserved for your traditional customers.

- Consider having internet sales handled by a different organization than your current sales team to avoid the temptation of sales providing additional value over that intended in a web-based offering.

- Discourage your traditional customers from cherry picking your offerings—buying some higher-value offerings through direct sales and turning to internet sales for lower prices on undifferentiated offerings. Consider policies that treat internet sales as spot sales which don't get included in your customer's volume rebates or loyalty programs: thus, their price of direct sales products might increase due to their lower volume as they shift towards internet purchases. Don't offer any sales assistance with internet purchases. In fact, let them know—visit frequency to them will be reduced commensurate with their lower direct sales volume.

- If reaching more customers is your goal, versus a low-priced channel, publishing a higher price can be effective. It sets the bar for non-contract customers and discourages price aggressive competitors.

Once you pinpoint your fair value, it's time to think about how you can not only achieve this fair price but also influence the market price upwards to achieve even further price. Let's go on the offensive.

Chapter 4: Behaviors for Doubling Your Price Increase Success

In my experience, supported by studies, most B2B businesses only achieve a 30%–40% success rate on their price increases until they learn and adopt best practices.[5] Many customers effectively negotiate the price increase down to lower levels than planned or even get full relief from the increase. While most suppliers blame their low success on a very competitive environment, it is far more likely to be due to the price-execution skill from leaders through sales. Low price-increase stick rate is a clear sign that you are not executing well. You can turn this around and double or triple your success rate with very practical, doable changes. I have coached hundreds of businesses through these changes, most in highly competitive markets, and all of them have been successful. The more they fully embrace the needed changes, the higher the success.

Setting a fair price, one the sales team has confidence in, and using the *best practice behavior guideline offensive skills* for raising price go a long way to improving your price increase success.

FAIR PRICE DEFINED

Fair price includes 1) getting a fair price or fair compensation for the value you deliver 2) achieving fair price increases and 3) influencing the market price to a higher, yet fair, level.

Setting a Fair Price Increase

The most successful price increases occur when market conditions are favorable for you as well as for your competitors.
Under favorable industry-wide conditions, it is far more likely that competitors will also be considering price increases—
perhaps leading you, perhaps following you. If competitors
raise price at roughly the same time, customers are more willing to accept increases, and additional competitors are more
apt to follow with their own increases. Companies that are
good at pricing continually monitor the market conditions.
When times are good, they quickly and proactively increase
price—to a fair price level—in a way that encourages others to follow. Likewise, when they see the market conditions
turning unfavorable, they quickly set their strategies and
tactics to proactively influence the market towards a slower,
smaller price decline. Doing this well can have enormous
impact on your profits—from influencing the market price
change *and* influencing the transition time between changing market conditions.

Favorable Market Dynamics

Favorable market dynamics include one or more of the following:

- **Tight or tighter supply/demand:** When supply and
  demand are tight across an industry, most competitors
  naturally consider raising price. The risk is small. Their
  customers can't easily leave as other competitors don't
  have excess capacity to fill their needs, and if they did,
  there are likely other customers looking for more supply.
  However, waiting for a tight supply/demand situation is
  not always necessary. If your industry has been running
  at a reasonable supply/demand level for some time then

suddenly begins to turn noticeably tighter (even if not quite tight), that may be enough positive change that competitors are ready to risk some volume and push price higher.

- **Shared pain/rising costs:** If raw material prices are rising across your industry, then all competitors are feeling their profits being squeezed lower. It is shared pain. Typically, they too are open to passing these higher costs along to their customer base. Yet, shared pain goes beyond just considering higher material cost. It can be from factors such as rising cost of freight, rising inflation, or rising costs of your manufacturing operations related to new environmental laws. Shared pain can be years of the industry suffering from very low or even negative earnings. If your competitors have low earnings, they are no doubt being tasked by their leadership to improve profits. As a result, they might be likely to follow you in an increase.

- **Competitor increases:** If your competitors begin increasing price, this might be an ideal time to increase as well. Quickly evaluate your situation and the market dynamics to determine if you have a fair rationale for increasing.

- **Market discontinuities:** Market discontinuities are unexpected events that result in the perception that you are a more attractive supplier often because another large supplier has become less attractive, unreliable, or unavailable. Examples include a significant unexpected shutdown, quality issue, or safety performance issue from a large competitor, as well as natural disasters that affect your competitors. If your offering is more in demand, even if only temporarily, this is a time to consider price increases. Be sure to do it in a fair and reasonable way. Becoming too bold will risk you being seen as a greedy opportunist and this may have long-term negative consequences for your relationships. Yet, not increasing your price is not fair to you. Attempt to find an appropriate balance.

- **Brand/value differentiation:** Any time you have a brand or value advantage, you should get a price premium. If your current premium is not sufficient, increase it.

- **Little or no increases in recent history:** If your industry has gone years without effectively increasing price, your margin is no doubt declining. Customers, if they are honest, know that you can't continue on this path without having to potentially reduce your innovation efforts or services and ultimately exit the market.

Additionally, the following conditions enhance favorable dynamics thus contribute to higher success or a bolder increase amount:

- **Growing market/favorable macro-economics:** When the market is growing and the economy is healthy, it is clearly an easier time to increase price. Your customers should be able to easily push the increases along to their customer base.

- **High-entry barriers/switching costs:** When customers can't switch suppliers easily (e.g., potential risks, switching costs, limited alternatives) or when it is very difficult/expensive for new suppliers to enter the market, you have more pricing power.

- **Low-cost percentage of customer's cost:** When your product is a small cost relative to the customer's overall costs, they are typically less price sensitive. Their buyers are often focused on their other larger purchases.

- **High-price ceiling:** The price ceiling refers to the highest point where if the market price where to exceed it, the market demand would decline. For example, if you sell polymers and the market price gets too high, the customer base might switch to a very different polymer, wood, or metal. If your price increase puts you near the ceiling—a low ceiling—then consider a less aggressive price increase.

Your pricing power is high if a few of these dynamics are occurring, but even just one favorable dynamic is often sufficient for success. With the right favorable conditions and the right behaviors from you, you are in an advantageous position to influence customers to accept your increase and for competitors to question whether they too should be increasing. You are positioned to win the game.

When a market tends to work such that competitors avoid price wars and raise price in similar amounts and times, it is often called a 'disciplined' marketplace. A disciplined marketplace is predictable and there is a broad sense of trust and fairness. Your aim should be to encourage behaviors that contribute to, rather than tear down, a disciplined market. The odds of having a disciplined market go way up when there is a handful, possibly three to five suppliers, that make up at least 50% of the market share. If your market is fragmented (no large players and many, if not hundreds, of small players), the odds of being successful in influencing the market price are lower. Yet, your behaviors will definitely influence your customers' aggressiveness.

Price Leadership

Should you lead price up or follow competitors? Should you go for the touchdown or punt? There is no one supplier that should be the implied price leader in each given industry. The value leader, followed by the player with the largest share, is typically thought of as the most effective to lead price. However, they are not the only choices. The price leader is situational; one competitor may lead the price up this quarter and a different competitor may lead price up in the following quarter. Any of the mid-sized to large suppliers can effectively lead price (i.e., suppliers with ~5% or higher market share). Price increases can be led with global price leaders or regional price leaders.

VALUE LEADER DEFINED

The value leader is generally one of the largest five players and is recognized as having the better products, service, innovation, or brand.

Even if you are a smaller player, less than 5% share, do not conclude that you can't affect the market price. You can, especially in the negative direction. And, you can contribute to upward prices when you quickly and visibly follow the price leader with your own price increases. Let me share two examples where relatively small players inadvertently influenced the market price down and later learned how to proactively influence the market price up.

Case Study 4.1:

One of my first business management roles in DuPont was leading a by-product commodity product. As a by-product producer, we were a relatively small player. On-purpose producers dominated this market. My company's main product was seasonal, consequently we had a large volume of by-product to sell in the first half of the year and very little to sell in the second half of the year. My predecessors significantly dropped price in the first half of the year to move as much product as possible, then disposed of any unsold material (at a cost to us). In the second half of the year, they were a very unreliable supplier as they had such little product to sell.

This was clearly disrupting the marketplace and hurting the market price. Furthermore, customers, rightfully so, didn't view us favorably. I needed to put strategies in place to become a reliable supplier and stop being a price disruptor. This required me to have a consistent supply and a stable customer base throughout the year. I achieved this through a series of (1) co-producer swaps with on-purpose suppliers (i.e., they took DuPont's excess product in the first half of the year and gave us product back in the second half of the year for a nominal fee), (2) adding additional storage, and (3) adding another distributor who had excess storage and a larger market reach. I followed this up with communications to our customers, as well as interviews to trade journals, indicating our actions to become a consistently reliable supplier throughout the year. I shared my view of the overall market supply/demand coming into balance or potentially becoming tight. I further indicated that as a reliable supplier our price would be increasing and remain stable throughout the year.

Quickly following these changes, competitors raised price. With our reliable supply, we acquired loyal customers and *no longer needed to dispose of excess product. In fact, we dismantled our disposal operation. With our higher volume and higher price, our profits went from a negative earnings position of several million to positive earnings close to $10 million dollars/year.*

Case Study 4.2:

I was coaching a $0.3 billion commodity business on their pricing strategy. This business was by far one of the smallest of the large players in their global marketplace. Their strategy had been to fully sell out their asset as they mistakenly believed that was a winning strategy for a commodity. Periodically throughout the year, when they had trouble selling out, they would ship their excess product to traders in Asia at a low price. The business rationalized this move by presuming that selling this product at any profit was better than not selling it at all. Furthermore, Asia was one of their smaller global markets, so they assumed it would have negligible impact on their major global markets. What they failed to see was that this behavior was negatively affecting their market price. Even being <10% market share, they were hurting market price. Their customers knew or sensed that they were volume-driven and negotiated aggressively for price. Competitors accurately assessed this volume driven behavior and became more aggressive. Their own sales force, never wanting to risk volume, easily fell into discounting. They had given up their pricing power and never realized it.

After a small team of our pricing consultants extensively reviewed the global markets and competitors, we convinced the business to change its strategy. Upon accepting our strategy, they no longer were driven to sell out the asset; they were driven to optimize earnings. They raised price, again and *again, using the best practice behavior guideline techniques shared in this book. The sales force was no longer afraid to risk volume; they had the courage, confidence, and conviction to push for their fair price or walk away. Their customers and competitors quickly realized they were serious and had conviction in moving price up even at the expense of losing volume. Competitors started to follow with price increases and earnings went up $35 million within the year. This business had taken its pricing power back.*

It is always riskiest to be the price leader, but if you are the largest player or the value player you almost have a duty to step up to this position. With this risk, you get the advantage of speed—higher prices sooner. The first supplier to announce an increase is positioned to most effectively influence the industry—they are setting the bar for the rest of the competitors. If one of your competitors announces before you, their announcement will affect the way you think about your own planned increase and how customers react to your price increases. If you were considering a 6% price increase, but the first competitor to announce came out with a 3% increase, you are going to have an uphill battle, or more likely, you will need to drop your increase to 3%–4%.

Support a supplier in your industry who acts quickly and leads boldly on price increases. Follow the increase immediately. Yet, if your competition is slow to announce price increases, or far too conservative, consider taking the lead.

Even if you are not positioned to influence the entire market price, your behaviors do influence your customers. Following these best practice behavior guidelines will ensure that you influence them toward less price aggression and more successful price increases.

⚒ BEST PRACTICE BEHAVIOR GUIDELINES: Offensive Skills

Creating trust and fairness in the marketplace includes three *offensive* practices:

1. Clearly communicate your intentions.
2. Be predictable—Walk the talk.
3. Be a value pricer.

Clearly Communicate Your Intentions

Good communications to the market are foundational for successful price increases. The market needs to know what price increase moves you are making and why. At a minimum, you need customer letters. Yet the more venues you use to communicate, the stronger your message will be heard and believed. Consider venues such as market announcements, updates on your website, trade journal articles, or market analyst interviews.

While price transparency is important, most of you will want to avoid communicating your actual prices and focus transparency on the price increase percentage or incremental amount.

⚒ Communications Guidance

- Clearly indicate your intentions and rationale.
    - *What products and markets are affected?*
    - *How much are they impacted (e.g., 5% increase, $2/unit increase)?*
    - *What is your rationale? What are the favorable industry dynamics?*

- Be viewed as fair and reasonable. The customer doesn't have to like it, but they should feel it is reasonable.

- Show respect for the customer. Indicate your value and commitment for the customer or the industry.

- Include a signature by the highest-level sales or business leader in your business. Allowing each salesperson to send and sign their own customer letters can create distrust. It leaves the customer wondering if they are being treated the same as all other customers. When the letter comes from the top, customers perceive that all customers are receiving the same treatment.

- Potentially include your view of the overall market conditions such as market trends and supply/demand projections.

- Put it in writing. Studies show that verbal communications are less trusted than written communications. It is fine, and encouraged, to also use verbal communications along with customer letters either before as a heads-up or afterward as a follow-up.

- Cover only your actions and your reasons. Don't indicate your views on what other competitors should or have done. This is an antitrust grey zone that might get you a penalty flag—one that comes with stiff consequences.

Frequently Asked Questions

- *Should a specialty product cite rising costs as a rationale?* Many business leaders believe that specialty product lines should not use rising raw material costs as a rationale for price increases—believing they should only value price. They worry that using rising cost as a rationale will result in them being perceived as a commodity player. I believe this is a big fumble. Specialty products are typically an enhancement of a commodity product; thus, they have a value-add relative to this base commodity. I have seen base commodity products increase price due to rising costs and end up exceeding the price of related specialty products. Specialty products should be considering their value-add to both in-kind competitors and not-in-kind (yet closely related) commodities. They will be leaving significant profits on the table if they don't increase price with rising costs.

- *If I increase price on the basis of raw material increases, won't I just have to give it back when my costs decline?* Fairness would dictate that you consider price drops if your costs later decline. Yet it is not a given. If you have other market dynamics working in your favor, such as a tight supply/demand situation, you can use this reason to avoid decreasing. Further, if your original announcement includes a second rationale such as, "Due to market tightness and…," or "In addition, we are increasing or enhancing our services," you will not have to give it all back.

  Additionally, there are risks in not passing along rising costs. Your earnings will be squeezed and you are still likely to be faced with customer price pressure if your costs drop in the future. When this happens, if your competitors fold to this pressure, you may have no choice but to respond as well.

- *Email or hard mail?* Either works but I am partial to email. Email has the advantage of being fast and more likely to be read. Furthermore, it can easily be forwarded to others. Thus, buyers can forward it to key people in their business or to their downstream customers/partners to aid them in pushing the price increase downstream. It also allows individual salespeople to add a personalized cover letter. Consider putting the actual letter into a PDF attachment so the letter is protected from editing or misuse. (See Figure 4.1)

Figure 4.1. Example Customer Letter

Dear Customer,

I'm writing to express our appreciation for your business and your loyalty. I also want to provide you background on the 8% price increase we're in the process of implementing. The unprecedented rise in energy costs and most of the key raw materials used to make chemical products have taken a heavy toll on the profitability of our business. Our raw materials have increased over 20% in the past two years alone.

We continue to diligently work on lowering our internal costs in a way that doesn't hamper our ability to bring the innovative solutions our customers expect from us. The squeeze in our profit margins makes it increasingly difficult to manage this balance.

I am ready and willing to discuss these and other issues with you in the spirit of partnership and mutual benefits. Again, thank you for your business and loyalty.

Sincerely,

John Smith, President

- *Should I announce a price increase range or a higher price than my intended target?* In the B2B world, 95% of the time, after announcing your price increase amount, customers begin pushing for relief. Oftentimes, you have a handful of customers whose price is exceptionally low and you want to increase their price even higher than the stated price increase amount. While a handful of other customers may already be at quite high prices and you are open to lesser price increase amounts for them. As a result, questions always arise on whether to announce a price increase as (1) a specific amount tied to your intended target amount, say 4%, (2) a slightly higher amount than your intended target amount (i.e., 6%) so most customers feel like they get a deal by accepting 4%, or (3) a range, say 4%–6% to allow flexibility with each customer. There is no one right answer; there are pluses and minuses to each approach:

- Announcing a specific amount tied to your intended target (e.g., 4%):

    Pluses: Providing your actual price increase target has the most integrity—you are asking for what you believe is the fair and appropriate increase. Overtime, it contributes to less aggressive customers.

    Minuses: This requires higher discipline and skill on the sales team to hold firm. If your past practice has been announcing high and accepting a lower increase, customers will be pushing hard for relief.

- Announcing a higher target than your plan (e.g., 6%):

    Pluses: Customers feel they got a deal if the salesperson drops to the targeted amount—which they are likely and happy to do.

    Minuses: You teach customers that pushing on price works—they get more aggressive in future negotiations. Customers may wonder if other customers got an even better deal. Additionally, it encourages the sales force to easily discount as they know their leadership's expectation is for a lower amount.

- Announcing a range (e.g., 4%—6%)

    Pluses: You can use the range to raise 'low-priced' customers further than other customers.

Minuses: Using a range implies room for negotiation and is likely to result in stronger customer push back. A significant percentage of the negotiations will default to the lower end (e.g., 4%).

In general, I lean towards using a range with the lowest amount being your intended target. If possible, I prefer to add a qualifier such as "4%—6% depending on product line." It combines much of the positives listed above while minimizing most of the negatives.

Additionally, referencing higher prices than your announced price can be beneficial—it influences customers towards believing they are getting a good deal without encouraging their aggressive push on price. You can do this with your customers through (1) discussing the upcoming price increase just prior to the official announcement indicating the business is finalizing the amount—possibly as high as 6%– 7%, (2) informing them your raw materials have increased 8%, or (3) pointing out similar industries are increasing 6%—8%.

If historically you have backed off your announced price increases, customers are likely to predict you will back off the next increase if they get aggressive. If you are serious about achieving a high stick rate this next go-around, you have a higher hill to climb. Consider making your announcement in a different way than you traditionally do as a subtle signal to customers that you are behaving differently this time. This might include releasing announcements to the news when you have not in the past, writing your customer letters in a different, possibly more detailed style, or having the letter come from your business president or CEO. The next case study illustrates these points.

Case Study 4.3:

In the 2006–2007 time frame, market dynamics for price increases were very favorable for the chemical industry due to the unprecedented rise in oil and feedstock prices. DuPont material costs were rising and the market environment was favorable for us to pass these costs along to our customer base. Within DuPont, we had some businesses that were still reluctant to pass along costs and some, that had already done a few increases, were concerned about yet another increase in such a brief time. However, it was clear that DuPont's contribution margin had been declining and would decline further if we didn't act boldly. I convinced our former CEO, Chad Holliday, to make a broad-based public announcement as well as send letters to customers indicating DuPont businesses would be raising prices due to these unprecedented costs. Chad was interviewed by analysts and made the evening news. This was the boldest price move in DuPont's history, both before and after this time, and we executed in a bold manner. Each business quickly followed up with separate announcements and/or letters to their customer base. This level of commitment from the top did wonders to boost the confidence and conviction in our sales force and to ease the potentially aggressive push back from our customers. Our success was exceptionally high. This approach was extreme, and I would not suggest using it too often, but the situation was exceptionally unique as well.

Internal Communications

Communications and preparation of the sales team is critical. Not only should they see external communications ahead of time, they should be given additional information. The more they understand and believe in the rationale, the better able they are to present these key points to customers. Provide the following guidance:

- **Questions and answers:** Anticipate typical customer questions and provide suggested answers.

- **Supporting data:** Provide any available supporting data such as copies of your supplier's price increase letters, publicly available price trends of raw materials (or precursors such as oil, natural gas…) or freight costs, producer price indexes for your industry, competitor's price increase announcements, and your historic price or contribution trend (in percentage change rather than absolute values—and only if declining).

- **Additional details:** Let them know which of the above information is approved to be either (1) shared/showed to customers but not left with them or (2) shared and copies left with the customer. Likewise, be clear about what data can't be shared or only shared verbally.

Antitrust Considerations

The way you communicate to the marketplace, especially about price, must be compliant with antitrust laws. You should seek your legal counsel's approval before issuing any communications. The United States and Europe have similar legal requirements and both are among the strictest regions in the world. Because of these laws, many legal departments are reluctant to do any communications beyond customer letters. However, this is a conservative approach and is likely leaving these companies at a competitive disadvantage.

I observed this same conservative approach with many of the DuPont businesses. At one point, I gave a presentation on this topic to the top 100 DuPont lawyers from around the globe. Initially, there was fast and furious push back from many of these conservative lawyers. Fortunately for me, the previous presenters just happened to be antitrust experts from

Washington. They quickly jumped into the dialog and put the lawyers' fears and concerns to rest. Additionally, the head of legal also supported my approach and counseled her staff to take a pragmatic approach. Her goal was not to avoid 'all possible risk thus disadvantaging DuPont' but 'to balance the risk/reward of any action while always staying within the law.'

ANTITRUST LAW DEFINED

The primary purpose of antitrust law (or competition law) is to promote fair competition for the benefit of consumers—essentially to ensure a fair playing field for competitors and customers. No collusion or information sharing among competitors is allowed on price, nor other sensitive market information, with the intent to distort competition—not directly nor indirectly through a third party. Public announcements are allowed if there is a plausible reason for doing so, such as reaching a large customer base. Price announcements should be done within 30 days or less to the effective date unless there is a plausible reason to announce with a longer lead-time. You should check the local laws of the region(s) you are operating within and always consult your legal department before making announcements.

Conspiring with competitors to set price, or 'signaling' competitors, is illegal. Legal departments are cautious about price announcements due to concerns that the announcement is done—or could be misinterpreted as being done—predominantly to 'signal' competitors in the hopes they will follow with their own increases. Unfortunately, they wrongly assume that customer letters are a sufficient means to communicate to customers. This is detrimental—a fumble. Here are some important reasons why making a price announcement is often needed:

- The most effective form of communicating a price increase, or other critical business information, is a public announcement, in writing and delivered or mentioned by a third party (such as an article in the Wall Street journal, or a news wire citing your written price announcement). It is most effective because it engenders the most credibility with the customer base—they are more apt to believe it and to believe it is fairly applied across all customers. A verbal announcement is the least credible.

- Customer letters are typically sent to the customer's procurement office. There is a risk this information may not get beyond the buyer and to the business leaders or the 'users' of your products within each company. You want this extended group to see the letter. Not only does it help to maintain the trust, but the announcement also helps the buyer internally defend the fair increase.

- It is often beneficial for your customer's downstream partners or customers to see the announcement. This gives your customers the coverage they may need to pass price increases along to their customer base.

- You want your message to reach potential new customers as well as your distributors, or other value chain partners, so they too understand your price increase.

- Announcements help boost the confidence and conviction of the sales force to implement the increase. It is a visible sign their leadership is behind them and it makes their negotiations easier.

- When the market understands your price action and perceives it as being fairly applied across all customers, you are more successful without risking volume.

Customer letters address and contribute to the sense of fairness of many of these issues but not quite as effectively as press releases. They should be used in addition to public announcements.

Be Predictable—Walk the Talk

One of the biggest fumbles I see is when companies announce increases then predictably back off these increases—rather than consistently enforce the increases. Over years, they have taught their customers to aggressively push them on price to get relief. They have taught their competitors that they are not seriously going to increase price. This undermines the courage of their competitors to raise their own price. The confidence and conviction of their own sales team suffers.

You must be committed to do what you say you are going to do. That means you must be willing to risk some volume and even walk away from some accounts. Even one or two rogue, unskilled, or unconfident sales resources can undermine your price increase efforts. The entire sales team must walk the talk. The first time you begin to change your behaviors to more committed behaviors expect hard pushback from your customers. They will push and push until they are convinced that you are committed to the increase. The good news is, overtime, the more you act predictably and with integrity, the more your customers and competitors are likely to believe you are committed to your increase; thus, the less price aggressive they will be. This applies throughout the year, even when you are not implementing a broad-based increase. Predictability must be an everyday occurrence.

If you lead the price increase, you must have patience. Competitors may take three to six weeks or more to follow. Buyers will try to convince you that no other supplier is increasing their price. They may stop ordering from you— often a temporary tactic. This can be a scary time that has the potential to undermine your confidence and conviction. Hold the line! The more you hold the line, the more likely your competitors will sense your conviction and follow with their own increase. However, if you begin to waver, the competition is likely to sense this as well, jeopardizing the likelihood of them following.

Case Study 4.4:

After informing the customer base that prices would be increasing, one customer stopped buying product from this supplier. After three weeks of no sales, the salesperson rescinded the price increase and the supplier began buying product again. A month later the salesperson's manager found out about the situation. The manager insisted the salesperson go back to the customer with the increase, hold firm and have patience. Once again, the customer stopped buying product in an effort to intimidate the salesperson. After nearly six weeks, when it was clear the salesperson was not going to back down, the customer accepted the increase and began buying again.

To reduce your risk, start your negotiations with smaller customers or your least attractive customers. Build your confidence with these accounts; if you lose volume it is likely to have little meaningful effect on your overall business. If needed, drag out your negotiations with large, tough accounts. Take a few weeks, and maybe several interactions to (1) build your confidence with less difficult negotiations so you can truthfully say, *"My other customers are accepting this increase,"* and (2) perhaps see evidence that other suppliers are starting to increase as well.

Be a Value Pricer

Value pricing goes beyond just getting a fair premium for your value. When it comes to price increases, there is an additional aspect that must be considered. You are going to face tough situations when you believe you must provide a smaller increase to maintain your share with certain accounts. Assuming you are correct, you must still demonstrate to these customers that you are a value pricer; nothing comes for free. If they want a lower-price increase, then there must be a 'give or take'.

Customer Gives: Get a longer contract, get access to customer data that proves your value proposition, get customer endorsements, get first rights to new application development products, get access to decision makers, get a favorable change in a price formula, get additional volume, or get a 30-day price-opener clause in your contract.

PRICE-OPENER CLAUSE DEFINED

A price-opener clause is a term in the contract that allows the supplier to reopen negotiations, strictly on the price, during the contract period. They are typically set as 30, 60, or 90-day price openers. A 60-day price opener means the supplier can tell the customer that their price will go up by X% in 60 days. The

> customer can then accept this increase, nego-
> tiate a different amount, or exit the contract if
> you insist on the increase. Price openers are
> frequently used in industries with volatile raw
> materials or supply/demand. It offers protec-
> tion to the supplier; thus, it allows them confi-
> dence in setting annual or multiyear contracts
> with volume commitments.

Supplier Takes: Reduce payment terms to 30 days or cash payments, extend lead-times, provide a lower value/quality product, remove services, exclude freight, ship to only one location, remove marketing or volume rebates, shift from 'off-the shelf' to 'make-to-order', offer weekday deliveries only, etcetera. If working with a distributor, who claims they need the lower price to compete in a specific end market, share the pain; both of you take a lower margin (and only for the portion of product going into this price-sensitive market).

In my experience, eight out of ten times you don't really need to lower your price, and the other two times, you probably don't need to change it as deeply as you think. There are also potential negative repercussions from backing off your increases—even for a justified reason. This has the potential to undermine all other negotiations. If competitors suspect you are backing off your increase, they will get more aggressive. You can be sure that most buyers will go out of their way to convince your competitors that you have not given them an increase. Additionally, salespeople often justify backing off the increase based on picking up share instead, yet customers rarely deliver on buying the promised volume.

The following case studies illustrate the three proactive behaviors of increasing price:

Case Study 4.5:

The CEO of a $0.9 billion revenue specialty & commodity business in the food industry called me for help. He had just taken over the business and was concerned about the past few years of near 'zero' earnings. I had guided the CEO's previous business to great pricing success, and he was hopeful I could do the same with this new business.

After a dozen interviews with sales reps and sales leaders, it was apparent that they didn't believe a price increase was possible. Their competitors were just too aggressive and they had tried before with little success. Yet, deeper analysis of the business showed there were favorable market dynamics for raising price; their raw material costs had risen significantly and they hadn't raised price in years. There were four other large competitors that were facing these same dynamics. Long story short, I persuaded the business to implement a 12%–24% price increase. Most of the products were targeted at 12% while a number of the more specialty products were targeted at up to 24%. After the initial shock to the salesforce, I convinced them that the increase was not only fair but critical for the health of the business. The CEO was on board and willing to walk away from customers unwilling to pay a fair price. With the right training, preparation, and price announcements, the sales force negotiated with confidence. They were enormously successful, achieving ~$100 million in annual earnings without losing volume. After a few tense weeks, the competitors followed with similar increases.

Case Study 4.6:

I worked with a highly commoditized business that had a handful of different product lines and was just slightly over

*$1 billion in revenue. They described their business as hav-
ing low and declining profitability, aggressive competition
from both in-kind and not-in-kind products, and very price-
sensitive customers, especially the traders. I provided price
training, followed by a few product line specific workshops to
set pricing strategies and tactics for the short and long term.
Throughout this six-week planning process, the commercial
leaders went from highly skeptical to excited to slightly scared
then back to excited as they began to successfully increase
price. Their confidence increased and in a few short weeks
of negotiations they had increased their annualized profit by
~$25 million.*

Case Study 4.7:

*I was training and coaching a large equipment company. They
were the market leader—both the value leader and the share
leader. For years, they had announced price increases, often
several times a year. However, as we looked closer at the fi-
nancials it became obvious that their average price was slightly
down over this five-year period—they had been predictably
backing off of their increases. Top leadership was pushing hard
for yet another increase. The sales team was skeptical, as they
should have been. After all, they had taught customers and
competitors that they don't follow through on their announced
increases. Without different approaches and practices by the
sales force, they were destined to repeat this behavior. We
dedicated three days to both train the sales force and set specific short-term and long-term strategies to increase price. The
sales team left with high confidence and conviction. Monthly
follow up teleconferences with sales indicated they were having
success after success with their negotiations. They were using
the practices and tools effectively. Their newfound confidence
continued and with it their success.*

I'm sure you see the similarities in these three cases. In fact, I could provide many more cases from specialty to commodity products and from diverse industries, but they are going to sound like the same story by a different name. In each of these case studies, the businesses were initially convinced they could not raise price—that their market was too competitive. They had all tried with no success in the past. In each case, once they began to change their own behaviors—in line with the best practice behavior guidelines—they amazed themselves with their success.

In addition to these guidelines which are focused on the external market, there are a few internal processes or practices that are foundational to support success.

Chapter 5: Building Courage, Confidence, and Conviction

I conducted a study across more than 50 businesses looking for the elements successful businesses utilized when raising price versus the elements exhibited by businesses with weak price increase success. Businesses where the sales force exhibited a high degree of courage, confidence, and conviction in their price increases had significantly higher price increase success. Three elements emerged as the key criteria for building this courage, confidence, and conviction. Additionally, the most successful businesses had a formal disciplined price-increase process.

Courage, Confidence, and Conviction

Companies that bolster their sales team with confidence—that the price increase is fair—and conviction to negotiate with high compliance are positioned to use their full pricing power. If the sales force lacks courage and confidence—if they are afraid to negotiate increases or become apologetic—they might as well walk into the customer waving a white flag of surrender. In no time, the buyer will uncover their uncertainty.

In fact, "Buyers' instincts are similar to dogs." Dogs have a keen sense of smell and they can smell fear. I can tell you, from personal experience, that when even so-called 'nice' dogs smell fear they can become very aggressive. I often hike alone, and I have a fear of large dogs. I can't tell you how many times I have been threatened or attacked by so-called 'friendly' dogs. On more than one occasion, a 'nice' dog has become so aggressive towards me that the owner was afraid to constrain it. When I am with friends, who have no fear of dogs, the dogs ignore them, running around them to snap at me. Clearly, dogs sense my fear. Recently, I got a lab puppy and am quickly losing my fear of dogs. As I gained courage and confidence with unknown dogs, not one dog has acted aggressively towards me. (FYI. Previous to getting a dog, I did try to hide my fear so the dogs would not know. They saw—or more accurately smelled—right through my act and continued their aggression).

So how does this relate to buyer instincts being similar to dogs? Buyers, even the nice ones, can quickly sense (if not smell) when a salesperson lacks genuine confidence and conviction in their price point or price increase. Once they sense this lack of confidence and conviction, they go in for the kill. They use every trick at their disposal to convince the salesperson to lower the price. They often keep at it until the intimidated salesperson drops the price. This dropping of price is just like giving a dog a treat. The buyer quickly learns to always act aggressively on price issues to get their treat of lower price.

Procurement best practices are geared toward under-mining the confidence of the sales representative. Buyers will do their best to convince you they

- will not accept the increase,

- don't deserve the increase,

- have lower priced offers—other competitors are not increasing,

- don't care about any of your 'extra value', or

- will shift their business elsewhere.

Buyers follow these practices because they work; they are tactics, often grounded in misleading statements, geared to test your conviction to your value, your price, and your willingness to walk away from volume. When you stand firm, with confidence, integrity, and with facts, you defuse their aggressive tactics. They begin to see that your company knows its value and is pricing fairly for that value. Further, they begin to feel that you are treating all customers the same. You are actually building trust.

Building this courage, confidence, and conviction in the sales team comes from three factors:

- **Fair Price:** Sales believing the price (or price increase) is fair given your value or your market conditions

- **Committed Leadership:** Sales believing that leadership is fully and truly committed to the increase (i.e., willing to risk volume) and that sales will be rewarded/ recognized for optimizing profits

- **Skills:** Sales having the skills to prepare for price negotiations, increase price, make smart price discount decisions, and execute in ways that builds customer relationships

Committed leadership was the top-rated success factor in the study. Done well, leadership can partially offset some skill weakness.

Fair Price

We addressed setting a fair price or fair price increase in earlier chapters. The litmus test for a fair price is whether the increase rationale feels fair and reasonable to the sales force. If it doesn't, leadership has some work to do.

Committed Leadership

It is no secret that raising price takes significant courage. My mental image of a price increase is walking up to a cliff's edge. If you walk too far, you fall off the cliff—a metaphor for losing volume. If you are afraid to walk close to the edge, you are not using your full pricing power. My mental image goes further to imagine the salesperson walking towards the cliff with a blindfold on. In the B2B pricing world, there is no definitive price you can calculate to know exactly where the cliff's edge is with each customer. The more skills you have, the more courage you will have to walk closer and closer to that edge. In fact, with more skills the edge actually moves further out. In other words, actions that influence towards less price aggressiveness with your customers and competitors move the market price higher.

Leadership sets the environment that enhances or destroys the courage to walk up to the cliff's edge. They must be willing to lose some volume! One of the top fumbles' a company can make is being unwilling to lose volume. Until you lose a little bit of volume, you will not know just how close you really are to the edge. I am not condoning losing a lot of volume or not carefully considering which markets and customers for which you will take this risk. You should take a prudent and well thought out approach. The good news is: the odds are great that you will not lose volume (or any meaningful volume) and you will gain confidence for negotiations with your toughest customers.

The most successful price increases I have seen have one thing in common. The top leader visibly stood up and clearly indicated (1) they expected extremely high compliance with the increase, and (2) they were willing to risk volume or walk away from accounts that were unwilling to pay fair price. These leaders meant what they said; they had no intentions of punishing a salesperson if volume was lost.

I have guided businesses through hundreds of price increases and nearly all of them experienced no or small volume loss relative to their high profit gains. I am only aware of two situations when a large, important account was lost and in each situation, the customer eventually returned. Both were very large price-sensitive accounts. In both cases, the businesses believed the customer when he said he would switch suppliers if the price increase was not waived. In both cases, the sales reps working hand-in-hand with their management agreed to hold to their fair price. They let the customer know that should they change their mind, they would be delighted to serve them in the future (at their fair price). In both cases, the customer did leave but returned in roughly three months agreeing to the fair price. Without committed leadership, the suppliers' salespeople would have heavily discounted these accounts on a continual basis.

In commoditized industries or industries where customers typically split their demand among a few large suppliers, you may see buyers immediately shift a few orders from one supplier to another, maybe even for a few months, as a tactic to intimidate you into thinking you had permanently lost share with them. Be patient and hold the line. The loss of a few orders is worth it if you get your price increase. If they value your offering (or their downstream customers do), they will be limited to the degree they can play this tactic. They will come back. In the long-run, you will be better off holding to your position.

Proactive behaviors established by leadership will strengthen this commitment:

- Visibly show pricing is a top & urgent priority.

- Walk the talk, consistently.

- Set aggressive targets & unwavering high expectations.

- Instill courage & conviction.

- Be willing to risk some volume.

- Invest in training & systems.

- Invest in communications—internally as well as value-based selling collateral.

These behaviors should be embedded in each contact with the team. Leaders are continually engaging with their teams in formal ways, such as group team meetings, monthly updates, quarterly reports, and celebrations or informal ways, such as phone calls and 'walking the halls'. Each of these written or verbal engagements are an opportunity to either reinforce their commitment to price or an inadvertent opportunity to undermine the organization's belief in whether leaders are serious about price. If they tell the sales team price is important, yet in each engagement they only ask about volume, share, and new accounts, they are sending conflicting messages. The sales force is likely to conclude that volume is king, and price is good only if it does not risk volume. During these engagements, leaders need to consciously ask about price as often as they do volume; they need to celebrate pricing wins as often as volume wins.

Rewards and Recognition

The sales incentive plan and any activities leaders do which recognize or celebrate good sales performance can significantly drive sales behaviors. They can hurt or help the ability to optimize price.

Some companies still compensate sales based solely on volume growth. A volume basis will hinder your ability to get your price (and therefore your profits) up. There is no personal gain for the individual salesperson to raise price, and there are significant negative consequences to their own pay should they lose volume. This has the potential to be a big fumble.

Sales compensation plans that are based on revenue growth are better than volume based; sales are equally compensated for a price or volume gain. Yet, it is not ideal as often a ~4% volume gain is needed to match the profit gain of a 1% price increase. There are better ways to influence the smartest price/volume decisions. A sales compensation program that includes a price or profit component is likely to drive the best behaviors for balancing price and volume decisions. This can be something such as a sales compensation based on contribution margin growth or a revenue based metric that has an adjustment based on price versus target price (or average price). Many companies opt for a compensation formula that is partially based on revenue and partially based on profit.

While I was leading DuPont's pricing, our sales teams were initially on salary. Many of the businesses switched over to 80% salary/20% variable compensation based on revenue growth. For years, we were unable to consider a profit-based program because we did not trust our financial systems to accurately assess the profit change at a sales territory level. This is a challenge for many companies. We were quite successful increasing price while sales were 100% salaried, yet we saw even greater improvement as we finally shifted to 20% variable pay. We overcame the natural bias of a revenue-based plan, to drive volume over price, through strong leadership and developing strong price negotiation skills. As our systems improved, businesses began to shift their compensation towards a profit component.

In addition to pay systems, recognizing and celebrating price successes can be very motivating. Some businesses recognize their top sales performers each month, each quarter, or annually. They use price or profit gain, along with development of new accounts as key selection criteria. They send out monthly emails highlighting these winners, post plaques on walls, or provide rewards such as gift cards or vacations. One company I worked with selected five salespeople/month who had either used a best practice pricing tool (from our training class) to make a smart decision or had achieved a price increase, then rewarded them with gift cards.

Skills

Throughout this book you are learning skills to enhance your ability and confidence to achieve higher price. Below are a few additional skills specific to success with price increases.

Building Customer Relationships

The most successful salespeople consciously work on building their customer relationships while implementing price increases. Improving or sustaining customer relationships involves taking actions so that the customer feels respected and fairly treated while perceiving empathy and honesty. It does not mean apologizing for the increase. These relationship-building actions occur in preparation for the increase, during the increase, and after the increase. Sales teams engender these feelings through clear and open communication of the fair price increase rationale, listening with empathy to the customer's concerns, helping them sell the increase internally or pass it along to their customer base, and staying close to the customer to provide support with challenges.

Preparing for Your Toughest Negotiations

Holding pre-negotiation preparation meetings is a great way to lay the groundwork. The sales team identifies customers who are likely to be their toughest negotiations. They try to anticipate the arguments or pushback from these customers, and collectively, they work on the best responses to these issues. They may even role-play the situation. It is critically important to prepare, plan, and practice ahead of the negotiations. The buyer will be prepared and may even bring along a few colleagues to strengthen his position. It is easy to become overwhelmed and intimidated in these situations. However, if the sales team is well prepared, they will not only be successful, but they will also present themselves (the company) as a value pricer with integrity.

✖ *Negotiation Planning Checklist*: It is helpful to prepare responses to the following questions before any tough negotiation—the first several are especially important during price increases:

1. *What are the toughest questions my customer might ask? About my value? About my price?*

2. *What will my responses be to these tough questions?*

3. *What will help customers understand and accept or internally defend the fair increase?*

4. *What is my pricing power with this customer— what buyer type are they (refer to Chapter 6) and how competitive is my offering?*

5. *What alternative offerings or concessions would I be willing to give this customer?*

6. *In exchange for my concessions, what concessions would I like to get from my customer?*

7. *What are my unique strengths relative to competition?*

8. How does my offering help the customer see a win in their business? Can I teach them something of value that leads them to my offering?

9. What are the underlying needs of this company and each of the people/roles I will be talking too?

10. What information do I need from the customer?

Disciplined Process

In addition to these supporting elements, successful price increases also require a disciplined process.

Designated Process Leader

A designated leader should be assigned to coordinate and guide the price increase process. There are many tasks that must be coordinated. Often the coordinator is a pricing leader, but it can be a sales operations leader or a sales manager. The key is to ensure they have the time and the skill to facilitate the process. They need not be a decision maker; but they must be a facilitator.

Disciplined Process and Metrics

The process includes the setting and alignment of price targets at a granular customer/product level, setting risk guidance, establishing the approval process, and issuing market communications. It also means monitoring the progress and success of the price increase which includes raising a red flag if things are not progressing as planned. Without close watch on the actual price negotiation results, it is easy to believe you are doing great things just to find out months later that your success rate was much smaller than expected. The biggest fumble I see in this phase of execution is salespeople holding firm on the increase with 80% of the customers—all the smaller customers. The few very large customers are getting no increase or a reduced increase. Since typically the top 20% of customers make up 80% of the businesses profits, if these large customers are given a pass, the total profits from the increase can quickly drop far below expectations.

Additionally, I have found it very helpful to add weekly or bimonthly short pulse check meetings into your process.

⚒ ***Pulse Check Meetings***: A critical time period is from the moment you notify your customers of a price increase and for the next month or two. This is a time when confidence can begin to waver. You are getting strong pushback and/or threats of lost volume from customers. You may still be waiting to see if competitors follow with increases while buyers attempt to convince you that competitors are not. This is a time for the sales team to teleconference 'huddle' once a week. The predominant aim of this 15–20 minute call is to build or sustain confidence and conviction in the sales force for high implementation success. Focus on the positives and successes, especially early in the call.

To keep it simple, consider a set agenda to guide the discussion:

1. ***Opening Comment:*** Kick it off with a very brief comment from the sales leader.
2. ***Success Sharing:*** Ask the group to share any success stories (or in the first few days of notification, any positive discussions). It builds confidence to hear that others are having success.
3. ***Tough Negotiations or Challenges:*** Ask if anyone who is facing a tough negotiation will share their situation. Invite the collective group to provide helpful suggestions.

4. ***Competitive Intelligence:*** Share any new competitive price announcements. Ask the group if they are seeing or hearing any signs competitors are also increasing.

5. ***Wrap It Up:*** Ask for any closing thoughts or concerns. Reiterate your expectations for high success.

During my DuPont experience, there was only one time I suggested a business pull back on their increase. This was in late 2008 when the large recession was just beginning to hit most industries. Earlier that year, I had advised all the DuPont businesses to implement their planned price increases in the first half of the year as it was becoming clear the world was heading for a recession. One business waited on their increase until the fourth quarter of 2008 just as market demand was dropping off. The market was soft. Competitors did not follow and customers needed to cut back on suppliers. We were going to lose share. The business quickly realized they had called a bad play and retreated.

NEGOTIATION TIPS

If the negotiation is not going well, consider these tactics:

- Drag it out: Don't give up too soon. Given time, competitors may also begin increases, your confidence might improve as other customers accept the increase, or your customer might begin to worry that you are looking at options to place your volume elsewhere.

- Adopt the new price during extended negotiations: Customers may try to drag out the negotiation for months, well past the increase 'effective' date. That's fine, but insist on having the new price go into effect on the announced 'effective' date despite the ongoing negotiation. You can always offer to rebate them if the agreed-upon price is less than the announced price.

- Require high-level management approvals for exceptions: This policy does three things: (1) it indicates to the customer how committed the company is to fully implementing the increase equally across all customers, (2) it helps preserve the relationship between the customer and the salesperson, and (3) it makes it less likely the salesperson will default to an exception.

Case Study 5.1:

In early October, a large customer put out a request for quote (RFQ) for the following year's supply. The incumbent business submitted a modest increase after years of no increase. They had always enjoyed a nice relationship with this customer from the decision makers to the users. It was a 100% share loyal account. Suddenly, they were informed that a new procurement team was formed and would be handling all negotiations. Almost immediately the buyer emailed a two sentence note to the supplier informing them their price was too high and they should submit a new price. The salesperson quickly responded to the email with a request to talk about their concerns so they could better meet their needs. Again the buyer sent a terse email, "No need to talk. Submit a lower price if you like. We are looking into other suppliers." The salesperson was worried and called me for advice. His company could not afford to lose this large customer and felt it was necessary to immediately respond with a lower price (albeit with a stripped-down offering). With a few questions, I learned:

- *Historically the customer was not a price buyer. They valued and utilized the suppliers' services. Even the RFQ listed the need for these services. Yet the salesperson was worried the new procurement team was comprised of price buyers.*

- *There was only one other competitor and it was likely they didn't have either the excess capacity to take on this large account or the ability to offer all services requested.*

- *The buyer indicated the price was too high, but he never said he had lower-priced options.*

The supplier was losing confidence in its pricing power. I needed to rebuild this confidence. It was clear to me this was a classic procurement tactic—pretending to be a price buyer to intimidate the supplier into dropping price. It was a bluff. The vagueness of the buyer's emails was a dead giveaway.

I recommended:

- *Relax; this buyer is just using classic tactics to undermine your confidence. They are giving themselves months to work you over. It is very unlikely they can make any decision on their own. In the end, they will need the decision makers and users to agree to switch away from you. This is highly unlikely given (1) your value to the users, (2) the likely lack of a good alternative supplier, and (3) your modest and reasonable price increase after years of flat pricing.*

- *Send them a short note that includes the following points: (1) our price is a very attractive, fair price, (2) we understand you will look at alternatives and we are confident you will find our value to be the right choice for you, (3) we can extend the quoted price for 30 days at which time we will send an updated quote based on our expected new 2018 price list, and (4) we have enjoyed a long relationship with you and value your business. We would like you to feel fairly treated. Please feel free to call if you would like a deeper understanding of our value and price. We would be delighted to discuss this with you.*

- *Reach out to the decision maker/users. Let them know the situation and check to see if they no longer value the services that come with your product. See if they will advocate for you with the buyer.*

- *Be confident. Let them see you acting without urgency or panic.*

- *As a backup plan, you can consider a slight reduction in your price increase if the customer is willing to do without some of the services you provide. However, it is highly unlikely you will need to do this, so don't proactively put it on the table in the early phases of negotiation.*

The business followed this plan. No surprise, once the customer's user was aware of the situation, they advocated to the procurement group on the supplier's behalf. The buyer eventually accepted the full increase.

You now have all the offensive basics for proactively increasing price and getting your fair price. Yet the most successful businesses, like the most successful football teams, excel at defensive skills as well.

Play 2:
Skill Drills to Build Your Game Plan

1. Think about your top undifferentiated product and your top differentiated product, and list for each product your value differentiators versus most competitors. Consider product features, as well as non-product features like reliability, security of supply, better sales force, brand, reputation, etc.

2. Given your value differentiators for each product, are you getting a fair premium with the market/customer segments that value your offering?
   a. What is your typical price premium?
   b. Do you have the sales collateral to effectively demonstrate your value to your customers?

3. For customers unwilling to pay a premium for your extra value, list the 'gives and takes' you can use if you must offer a lower price.

4. What favorable industry pricing dynamics exist (or will in the near future) which might be used as a rationale for increasing price?

5. What best practices or actions do you, or your business, do well relative to increasing price?

6. What best practices or actions do you, or your business, not do well in price increase execution?

7. If you are about to implement a price increase, identify the top few customers that will be your toughest negotiations and list their likely negotiation arguments or tactics. What counter arguments or tactics can you use to enhance your success?

8. What actions or behaviors will you, or your business, do differently going forward?

PLAY 3:
THE SKILLS FOR SMART
PRICE-DROP DECISIONS

Even professional football teams can't always go for a touchdown. Sometimes they must go for the field goal and at times they need to punt. For certain, they must play defense. The best teams consistently excel at defense. The better they are on defense, the more time they are able to play offense. There are a lot of parallels to B2B pricing.

In B2B pricing, there will undoubtedly be times when discounting the price is necessary. Most suppliers have encountered aggressive competitors who were targeting their customers. You need to be as skilled in defensive moves as offensive moves. In fact, maybe more skilled. You may only increase price once or twice a year, but you are facing price pressure daily.

Buyers are adept at trying to convince you they only care about price. For some of them, that is true. For others, likely the majority, that is only a tactic. They are willing to pay a premium for extra value despite what they say. Buyers have professional skills aimed at undermining your confidence. They are good at it! I see far, far more discounting than is necessary, and even the needed discounts go far deeper than required.

The following chapters are focused on helping you make smarter price-drop decisions every day. These decisions require you to evaluate many factors to make the best decision. They can be complex, but I will share practical tools that can turn these complex decisions into easy decisions. Understanding different buyer types, your pricing power with each, and strategies to effectively deal with each buyer type is an essential foundational skill. Managing well in the face of aggressive competitors or unfavorable market conditions will defuse downward price pressure. Along with solid decision-making, the techniques for mastering the conversation and building a win-win agreement must be employed.

Bolstering the decision-making process, sharpening the conversation, and engendering trust are the guideposts for smart *defensive* price-drop decisions. Yet, there may be a few circumstances when an *offensive* price-discounting strategy might be a smart decision. In football terms, this would equate to a team's strategy of winning based on having successful interceptions, play after play. It's possible under certain conditions, but most competitors will adjust their game plan to prevent your success.

It's time to block and tackle.

Chapter 6:
Managing Different Buyer Types

Most of your buyers may sound like price buyers, but let me assure you the odds are high they are not. Just think about your past negotiations for a minute. You have likely won some business when you had the highest price, and have lost some business despite having the lowest price. One of the most important skills to master is determining the type of buyer you are dealing with. *Are they only about price or do they value other features*? This is a key determinant in how much pricing power you have. The more power you have, the less you need to discount. The buyer type is also a key determinant of how attractive this customer is to your business. Understanding your most attractive customers, and conversely your least attractive customers, is critical in tight markets (i.e., *which customers to walk away from?*), in preparing for loose markets (i.e., *which customers to shift more of your product to?*) and in implementing price increases (i.e., *which customers to take the most risk with?*).

During my tenure at DuPont, I coached many businesses in identifying their different buyer types and needs, segmenting them into customer needs-based groups followed by differentially treating each segment. We used the most sophisticated, in-depth techniques (e.g., discrete conjoint analysis) to identify the segments. We did this with specialty and commodity businesses in all regions of the world. As we began, every business and every region felt they had unique and different buyer types. However, a pattern emerged that held for all businesses.

In each business and region, the same four types of customer needs-based segments or buyers emerged: the relationship buyer, the price buyer, the value buyer, and the convenience buyer.

IDENTIFYING BUYER TYPES

Relationship Buyer

The relationship buyer values having a connection or bond with you. They are the most loyal customers and easiest for you to do business with. Often, they are your favorite and highest-priced customers.

- **Needs:** They want extra support with their issues or challenges. This may be in technical assistance, regulatory support, marketing assistance, or other areas such as reliability of supply or logistics. It is not uncommon that the attributes they value from you are less about the product and more about your services, responsiveness, and the entire customer experience. They typically have limited internal skills in your area of expertise.

- **Interaction:** They want to interact with you and are happy to take your calls, have a meeting, or go to lunch. They are the 'family and friends' of the business world. Some relationship buyers, especially those from family run businesses, enjoy attending events as your guests and feel honored to meet your top leadership. They like feeling they are important to you.

- **Loyalty:** Relationship buyers are the most loyal type of buyer. As long as you treat them fairly and meet their needs, they are unlikely to 'shop around' for other options.

- **Number of Suppliers:** They typically sole source or have one primary supplier with a backup supplier.

- **Decision Maker and Information Access:** You have easy access to the decision maker, or in the case of the 'Mom and Pop' customers, the owner. They are open about their business and their needs.

- **Negotiation Process:** The procurement department is not heavily involved although they may be brought in at the final stages to conclude the deal. Rarely, do they hold a formal bidding process or even compare other alternative suppliers once you have proven yourself. Their decisions can be very quick if the owner is making the decision or if they are renewing your contract, however, in larger firms, if the buyer is considering another supplier, the decision can be quite slow because the buyer does not have decision authority. He or she must check with the leaders or users in their company who are receiving the value. That's good for you as these folks are likely to be your biggest fans.

- **Games:** Relationship buyers rarely play games. They are open and honest with you and expect this same behavior from you.

- **Price/Value Trade-Off:** They will pay a premium for your extra value. They are likely your highest-priced accounts.

- **Customer's Emotional Involvement:** Emotions can run high if a relationship buyer feels unfairly treated. Just like a family member or close friend would take a slight from you more deeply than from a stranger, so too does the relationship buyer. They like this relationship and may become upset if they think something might undermine it.

- **Your Pricing Power:** Your power is very high. As long
  as you continue to perform well, deliver the value they
  need, and treat them with fairness and respect, you
  are golden. Your relationship is even strong enough
  to weather some 'performance issues'. Just be sure to
  treat them well during these times and don't abuse the
  relationship.

Price Buyer

Just as their name implies, price buyers are all about price.
They are the opposite of the relationship buyer. You have less
pricing power with this segment and often, you need to consider discounting. If the relationship buyers are your favor-
ites, the price buyers are your least favorite.

- **Needs:** It's 99% all about price, price, and price—who
  has the lowest price. However, in many industries, price
  buyers often have a second (possibly distant) need,
  for reliability of supply, consistent quality or perhaps
  short-lead times. If they (or the industry) have just gone
  through a significant shortage of product, then reliability
  and security of supply may be of higher importance for
  some time.

- **Interaction:** Their motto tends towards: "Don't call me,
  I'll call you." They only call if they are looking for lower
  price, need something from you, or want to take you to
  task if there has been a performance issue.

- **Loyalty:** Price buyers are rarely loyal; they are open to
  switching for lower price. Yet, if your product is very
  important to their business, or they perceive a real risk
  in moving away from you, they will not switch easily.
  They prefer to stay with you and need a compelling
  reason to switch, beyond a small price gap.

- **Number of Suppliers:** They typically have multiple suppliers and they do shop around for lower price options.

- **Decision Maker and Information Access:** You are blocked from the decision maker; probably from everyone other than the buyer. They provide you with limited information about their business and needs. They may believe that providing you information will be used against them in the price negotiation.

- **Negotiation Process:** Expect a formal, disciplined process, possibly a request for quote (RFQ) or even a reverse auction. They are likely to add specific offering requirements and/or performance requirements into this request. The offering requirements weed out unsatisfactory suppliers or influence the selection towards their preferred supplier. The performance requirements may have penalties associated with poor performance, and at minimum, they can use your poor performance against you in future negotiations. They make fast decisions because the selection criteria are simple (essentially price) and the buyer is likely the decision maker. He or she has no need to consult with others before deciding.

- **Games:** Do expect games and misleading comments. They will try to convince you they have a lower price option even if it is not really a viable option. They may threaten to pull their volume from you unless you meet their price demands. This may or may not be true. If you are not their primary supplier today, they may suggest that you can win their business (or much more of their business) if only you would lower your price. They are often doing this with no intention of giving you this volume. They just want your lower price to pressure their primary supplier into dropping their price.

- **Price/Value Trade-Off:** In general, they are not willing to pay for extra value. Price is their key decision criterion. However, a slight premium is possible if you are selling an important or risky product to them and/or reliability, security of supply, quality, or short lead-time matter to some degree.

- **Customer's Emotional Involvement:** Price buyers do not get emotionally involved. If you raise their price, they can always shift to a supplier with lower price. After all, they claim your features are no different than the next guy's. Yet, be aware that some price buyers will 'act' mad to intimidate you into lowering your price. This is not a genuine emotional response. If it were, perhaps they are not really the price buyer they profess to be.

- **Your Pricing Power:** You do have some pricing power if you are the incumbent supplier. Your pricing power is the lowest with this group yet they still prefer to stay with the incumbent. If your offering is important to them, or they perceive a risk if they switch, your power increases.

Value Buyer

The value buyer sits somewhere between the price buyer and the relationship buyer. They value some of your features but not all. They tend towards loyalty but are also weighing their options.

- **Needs:** They value more than just price and are willing to pay for this value. Yet, they are unwilling to pay for other features. For example, they may be willing to pay more for application development/custom products but will not pay for troubleshooting or other technical support. Others might value your brand (and their ability to co-brand their products) but are unwilling to pay for service. Yet others might value your reliability and security of supply but are not interested in custom products.

- **Interaction:** While they are not as social/interactive as relationship buyers, they will interact with you especially around value discussions.

- **Loyalty:** Value buyers tend to be loyal as long as your value/price balance seems fair to them. They will, however, compare and consider other suppliers; always weighting the value/price by supplier along with the risk of switching suppliers. If you are their current supplier, you have a leg up. They need a compelling reason to switch.

- **Number of Suppliers:** They typically split their volume between two suppliers: their primary 'go to' supplier and a secondary supplier.

- **Decision Maker and Information Access:** Initially, you do have access to the decision maker(s) and they will answer some of your questions. This information is often limited to what they think you need to know about their business or information that best serves them.

- **Negotiation Process:** Initial negotiations may be done with the users or decision makers, but as the negotiations start to get serious, procurement may step in and take over. Suddenly, you are being blocked from decision makers and additional information. The deal, which you thought was near complete, now turns into a formal process. Procurement may even start an

RFQ or begin taking bids from other suppliers. This is most often done to put price pressure on you, their preferred supplier. Negotiation decisions are the slowest with this segment. They have a lot of price/value trade-off decisions to make and often there are many users/decision makers that must weigh in on the decision.

- **Games:** Value players undoubtedly play games. Their two primary games are to try to convince you (1) they are a price buyer—they don't value your extra features and are unwilling to pay for them, and (2) they have viable, lower-priced alternatives which they will switch volume to if you insist on high price.

- **Price/Value Trade-Off:** They will pay a premium for select features of your service or product, but it is not blind loyalty. They must believe the extra value for the premium price is fair or they will consider lesser value suppliers.

- **Customer's Emotional Involvement:** Value buyers will get somewhat emotional during price-increase negotiations. They value you and are worried they may have to shift their volume to a lower-priced supplier. They would definitely prefer not to switch suppliers; they recognize there is risk in switching.

- **Your Pricing Power:** You do have pricing power and it is fairly strong. They prefer to stay with you.

Convenience Buyer

The convenience buyer values the fast, easy, no-hassle buy. It's not about price. Perhaps it is an emergency and they need a product right away or perhaps you are the closest store front, warehouse, or manufacturing site to their location. In the case of emergencies, any of the other buyer types (price, value, or relationship) can turn temporarily into a convenience buyer just to manage through the emergency. They need to fix their problem fast and price is not at the top of their minds. In the B2B world, we see less convenience buyers. Many industries will not even have this group; however, nearly all industries have other buyer types that turn into convenience buyers in emergencies.

- **Needs:** Their primary needs are fast, hassle-free and easy to do business with—especially in emergencies. They need product (or services) fast and don't have the time or energy to jump through bureaucratic hoops to get it.

- **Interaction:** Interactions are limited to when they need services.

- **Loyalty:** Convenience buyers are very loyal if you remain fast and relatively easy to work with.

- **Number of Suppliers:** They often are sole sourced or at least have their primary 'go to' supplier.

- **Decision Maker and Information Access:** You have easy access to the decision maker and any key pieces of information you need to supply them.

- **Negotiation Process:** The negotiation is often an informal quick process. They want it fast and easy on both sides.

- **Games:** Convenience buyers rarely play games; it takes too much time and hassle.

- **Price / Value Trade-Off:** They will pay a premium and they don't shop around.

- **Customer's Emotional Involvement:** Emotions can run high at times for several reasons: (1) If it is an emergency, then emotions are likely tied to how fast you can meet their needs. (2) If the customer works with you because you're the easy, fast choice, they may get emotional if you are raising the price to an unfair level or 'taking advantage' of them. (3) They might be 'stuck' with you if they have invested in a pipeline or piece of equipment tied to your product.

- **Your Pricing Power:** Your power is very high. They are often not price sensitive and you are the easiest one for them to do business with (at least at this moment).

Other Tips

Depending on the business or region, the percentage of customers that fall into each buyer type vary. For example, overall 20%–25% of B2B customers are typically price buyers with commodity businesses averaging slightly higher (25%–35%) and specialized businesses slightly lower (15%–20%).

A value buyer in one business might have high value for your new, innovative products. In another business, the value might be tied to co-branding arrangements. You must understand specifically what each buyer group values so you can enhance the experience while removing effort that is not valued or being paid for. The good news is that, independent of the actual feature(s) the customers value, the pricing tactics for dealing with this type of buyer are the same.

The most difficult situation is when a customer buys several different products from you and is a value buyer for some products (likely your specialty grades) and a price buyer for others (likely your undifferentiated products). Under this scenario, you have slightly more power on the undifferentiated products than you would with a traditional price buyer.

They will lean towards keeping with one supplier.

Table 6.1 summarizes these different buyers' traits. Additionally, there are two subsets of these segments that also need to be considered: the 'Price-buyer pretenders' and the 'Play-you-for-a-fool buyers'.

✖ Table 6.1. Buyer Type Identification Markers

	RELATIONSHIP BUYER	VALUE BUYER	PRICE BUYER	CONVENIENCE BUYER
Loyal				
Want to Interact				
Emotionally Involved				
Multiple Suppliers				
Decision Maker Access				
Multiple Decision Makers	Unless Family Owned			
Formal Bid Process		Often But Not Always		
Fast Decisions	Unless Family Owned			
Importance of Value				
Switching Costs/ Risks				
Willing to Pay for Value				

Key: Dark grey is high correlation, light grey is good correlation & white is low correlation

Price-Buyer Pretenders

Price buyer pretenders are buyers that aren't price buyers yet want you to believe they are. They are sheep in wolves' clothing. They want you to think they are the big bad price buyer who will only work with you at discounted prices. In reality, they do value you and will pay a premium if necessary. They are value buyers in disguise. This tactic of pretending to be a price buyer works wonders for them. Many salespeople fall prey to it and provide unnecessary discounts.

- **Recognizing a price-buyer pretender:** There are several 'tells' for recognizing this pretender. Let's start with the assumption that you are the incumbent supplier, or at least well known to the customer. You are in the middle of a negotiation with the decision maker and things are going along well. You're having informal discussions about needs and you believe the customer is leaning your way. In fact, you believe you are about to close the deal. Suddenly procurement takes over the negotiation. The decision maker is no longer returning your calls or emails; he forwards them to the procurement group. You thought you were one of a few suppliers, if not the only one they were talking to when suddenly new suppliers are added late in the game. Procurement is threatening to put the work out for a formal bid and they seem to be slowing down the process. All these actions are done to make you nervous, undermine your confidence, and get you to lower the price unnecessarily.

- **Strategies for Dealing with A Price-Buyer Pretender:** Let's look at six tactics pretenders use in an effort to get lower price as well as counterbalancing plays you can employ to block them.

    Pretender Tactic #1: They claim, *"I only care about price."*

    Response: The quickest way to defuse this tactic, as well as to uncover whether they really are a price buyer is to offer to take something away from your offer so you can provide them a lower price. The trick is to take away something that you believe they really value. If you believe they value your product's high purity, say something such as, *"If we could supply a lower purity product at a lower price, would you be interested?"* If they respond with, *"No, I need the higher purity,"* then you have your answer. They do value your offering and they are not as price sensitive as they claim.

Pretender Tactic #2: They attempt to convince you they have shifted share away from you. They stop ordering from you for weeks—often just depleting their inventory or shifting one or two orders to another of their other suppliers (without ever letting on to the other supplier that they have temporarily shifted share to them.)

Response: Your tactic should be patience. Wait it out at least 4—6 weeks to see if this behavior continues.

Pretender Tactic #3: They delay the negotiation to unnerve you. They are hoping you will view this delay as disinterest in your offering or that they are in serious negotiations with other suppliers.

Response: Your tactic should be to delay even more; unnerve them! Let them worry about whether you are selling your offering to other customers more willingly to pay fair price. This works especially well if you have limited product or limited resources for services.

Pretender Tactic #4: After delaying the process for weeks, they call you in and try to force you to provide a decision on the spot or return with your 'best price' offer within a very short-time period. Both are artificial deadlines. They likely provide a contrived reason for needing this fast decision such as, *"I have to pres ent my options to management tomorrow afternoon!"* They are hoping you are unnerved enough to react without having the time to be thoughtful.

Response: Resist agreeing on the spot. Slow down. You need a cool head before thinking about discounting options. If you are their preferred supplier, they will not let this 'rush tactic' take you out of the running. The speed of response is very meaningful. Fast responses can signal you are desperate while slow responses signal 'you have the power' and aren't going to be rushed into an unfair agreement.

Pretender Tactic #5: Procurement threatens to go out for bid if you can't come to agreement on a lower price.

Response: First, show no fear. Do exhibit confidence in your value and price relative to their other choices. Let them know this will delay the process and there are risks to delaying. For example, suggest you may place your volume with another customer or your price is only good until the new price list comes out. Set a time window on your bid (e.g., it is only good for 15 days).

If the formal process takes extensive time to prepare, such as often occurs in service or large equipment buys, inform them this extra effort may result in an increase in price. Suggest that it might serve both parties better if you could work on a mutually agreeable solution—one that lowers their price but fairly compensates you as well. If this doesn't work, consider one of these options: (1) ask them to compensate you for your effort in preparing the bid—which you will reimburse if you win the bid or (2) walk away from the deal—tell them something such as, "*We value your company and our relationship. Please call me if you would like to better understand why our price is fair and attractive for the value we deliver. We would be delighted to discuss this with you.*" Then reach out beyond the buyer, to the users, in a subtle way, to see if they might intervene on your behalf to the buyer.

Pretender Tactic #6: They insist on adding performance criteria into the contract. If you don't hit the performance level there is a price penalty. This tactic is not just limited to pretenders; price buyers utilize it as well.

Response: Tell them you are open to considering these criteria provided they go both ways; risk and reward. If you should exceed the performance level, you should be awarded higher price.

Playing-You-for-A-Fool Buyer

At times, you reach out to customers whom you have never served before, or these customers reach out to you, for a quote. They imply their volume is yours if you come in with a low enough price. *Are they serious or are they just using you to get a low-price offer to use against their current supplier(s)?* The last thing you want to do is go through the hoops to pull together a low-priced offer if you have virtually no chance at getting the business. Not only is it a waste of your time and energy, but it has the potential to start a price war. Surely, the potential customer will take your low-price bid to their preferred supplier(s) and demand they match it to keep this business. *So how do you recognize whether you are being played for a fool?*

- **Red Flags:** If this customer has been loyal to another supplier for years, this is a big red flag. Loyal customers rarely switch suppliers unless the supplier has been underperforming. Other red flags are the inability to get access to the decision maker or to get useful information to scope your offering; this is especially true if the supplier knows little about your company.

Being brought in late into the bidding process is another sign you are not a serious contender.

- **Green Flags:** If the customer is dissatisfied with their incumbent supplier, you have a real shot to displace them. However, if this is the case, you don't need to drop your price—offer your product at fair price. Additionally, if you have noticeably superior value you have a shot at winning—once again, do it at your fair price.

POLICIES & TACTICS FOR EACH BUYER TYPE

Policies and Tactics for Relationship Buyers

The overriding tactic in dealing with relationship buyers is to build the relationship—help them feel fairly treated and valued by your company. Offer them extra support such as technical services, training, or market insights. If reasonable, use dedicated sales, customer service representatives, or technical support resources so you can build a relationship at multiple levels. If they are large enough, build relationships at the upper management level: your leaders to their leaders.

- **Offering:** Offer them a full bundle of products and services. Don't nickel and dime them for every little extra request. Be easy and flexible to do business with. Many relationship buyers, especially family-owned businesses, really value being invited to events (e.g., golf outing, Nascar race, dinner, sporting event) or meetings with upper management. It is a highly effective way to help them feel valued.

- **Pricing and Discounting:** Avoid discounting or negotiating. You don't have to. They will pay premium prices and are likely to be among your highest priced accounts. Long-term contracts with these great customers can be a good idea.

- **Other:**

  - If you do run into a performance problem (e.g., quality issue, supply issue), these loyal buyers will be your most forgiving customers. Nonetheless, this is a time to work on the relationship and keep your communications high. Offer a genuine apology and be open and honest about how your company is resolving the problem going forward.

  - Don't target the loyal accounts of your competitors unless you deliver superior value and are not planning on discounting. These loyal customers of your competitors are highly unlikely to switch suppliers for price. At best, they will invite you to offer a low price then turn right around to their loyal supplier, giving them the right to keep the business at this price. In the end, you will not get the volume and you will have created a more aggressive competitor. However, do periodically visit your competitor's loyal accounts and begin to build a relationship. Let them know, you are willing to step in should their loyal supplier have supply issues. Sell your value and hold true to your fair price. If their primary supplier has performance issues, you want them thinking about you as their top alternative. If it happens, you will not need to discount to get this business.

Policies and Tactics for Price Buyers

You will need to offer a low-price option. The key is to make sure the offering is of lesser value than your offering for high-er-paying segments.

- **Offering:** Strip down the offering: remove services or product features they are unwilling to pay you for. Consider low-priced ordering or selling models such as online ordering or very low touch sales. Only sell in bulk such as full truck loads. Exclude them from getting select products or services even if they would be willing to pay a surcharge. As an example, don't allow them access to your custom products but do allow them to pay a surcharge for short lead-time deliveries.

- **Pricing and Discounting:** Discount only if you have stripped down the offering. If you do have something they value, even slightly, like reliability or short lead-times, get a slight premium. Discounting is always risky so it is best done if you have a 'fence' between these types of buyers and your other buyers. Do nickel and dime this segment. Add surcharges for any extras they may want such as small order size, emergency delivery or services. Finally, be ready to walk away. This business might not be worth it due to the smaller profit, the risk of creating an aggressive market, and tying up your supply with low prices. Further, walking away can be the action that results in the buyer backing off their price demands. Here is one comforting thought: if you lose a price-buyer account you can nearly always buy your way back in later.

FENCES DEFINED

A fence is a metaphor for putting an obstacle between different buyer type segments so that you can offer a low-priced offering to one segment and not have it bleed over into another higher-value segment. Movie theaters use age as a fence. Children and senior citizens are offered discount prices that are not available to the rest of the population. In B2B, a fence might be varying brand choices or different channel choices like face-to-face sales versus online sales.

- **Contracts:** Don't sign contracts, or if you must, at least make them short term. Consider adding price openers of 30, 60, or 90 days so you have an opportunity to raise price if the market conditions get more favorable or you have more/better customers wanting to buy this material. Put a limit on the volume you are willing to provide at this low price; even consider putting a monthly volume cap at this price.

- **Other:** If you are not the primary supplier to this customer, be sure you get a higher price than the primary supplier since you are selling less volume. Additionally, be sure to charge a premium to bail out this primary supplier when/if they are in trouble (thus the need for monthly volume limits).

Always test to assure yourself that the buyer is truly a price buyer and not a value buyer in disguise.

Case Study 6.1

I recently worked with a company in a reasonably tight market but they were foreseeing a loosening in the market in about six months. One of our strategies was to shift volume away from price buyers and move it to customers who truly valued this supplier and their better reliability. The supplier went to several of their price-sensitive customers, suggesting not only price increases but a drop in committed volume. To their surprise, these customers fought for the higher volume and were willing to pay even higher prices for this incremental volume. They recognized that this supplier had the highest reliability in the industry—and after several recent supply problems from other suppliers—they had a new found value for reliability.

Policies and Tactics for Value Buyers

Offer choices to these buyers as well as assist them in comparing your offering/price to their other alternatives. Clarity on your value proposition and your ability to effectively articulate this value proposition will be important (see Chapter 3).

- **Offering:** Unbundle your products and services. Offer them different value choices at different prices—varied brands or just the inclusion or exclusion of certain services. Try to align your offer to their specific needs. Remove features that are unimportant to them. Quantify or prove your value to the best of your ability. Help them compare your offering, value, and price to other competitors' offerings, values, and prices to help you close the deal. *These buyers are likely making these comparisons anyway, so why not ensure they have a valid comparison that showcases your offering in the best light?*

- **Pricing and Discounting:** Align the price to the offering value. If they want a higher-value offering, the price must also be higher. Use surcharges for any extra services or features they request beyond the agreed upon offering. If you are forced into discounting, always be sure to get something in return or to take something away. You must consistently be seen as a value pricer.

- **Other:**

  - If the customer agrees to behaviors that reduce your costs (e.g., ordering in full truck loads, ordering only once a month) then reward them—share the savings.

  - Once you have established a relationship with the buyer, try to upsell them on additional products or services. This upsell should be based on a value discussion. Getting beyond the buyer to your customer's decision makers or users of your offering is the best place to make the sale. Furthermore, if the buyer ever threatens to shift volume away from you, you will want to reach out to these roles. Re-sell your value and play up the risks of shifting away from you. The users of your offering—the ones that receive the value from your offering—are the ones most likely to go to bat for you with their procurement team.

  - If you are negotiating with a potential new customer that you suspect is a value buyer, you have an uphill climb. You need to demonstrate you have real value to win, especially if you are not well known to this customer.

Policies and Tactics for Convenience Buyers

As with relationship buyers, convenience buyers are easy to negotiate with. You can offer full price or even an upcharge for emergency or custom service. Just be fast and easy to work with.

- **Offering:** Provide the offering that best meets their needs without going through customized choices. If in doubt, offer the high-value offering.

- **Pricing and Discounting:** Don't discount or negotiate. In fact, include an upcharge if their request is out of the ordinary. For example, they are not under contract with you, they have an emergency and need product sooner than your typical lead-time, or they typically buy 1000 tons a month and now need 2000 tons in one month.
- **Other:** They are often buying from you because of the convenience, so make the entire customer experience fast, low-hassle, and easy.

Table 6.2 summarizes the policies and tactics for different buyer types.

Table 6.2. Buyer Type Policies and Tactics

	RELATIONSHIP BUYER	VALUE BUYER	PRICE BUYER	CONVENIENCE BUYER
Offering	Bundle	Unbundle	Stripped Down	Bundle
Price	Value-Price; Don't Discount	Value-Priced, Slight Discount	Discount, Small Prem.:Rel/LT	Full Price
Concession		Gives or Gets	Gives or Gets	
Extras	Don't Nickle & Dime	Upcharge	Charge/Don't Allow	
Contract	Long		Short/Price Openers	
Relationship	Build Relationship	Value based	Don't Invest	
Competitors	Don't Target their Loyal Customers	Help Comparisons	Premium to Bail Out	Emergency Charge
Other	Be Flexible & Easy		Ready to Walk Away	Be Fast & Easy
			Bulk Shipments Only	

Now that you have classified your customers and determined your game plans for each segment, it's time to tackle the defensive moves needed to manage aggressive competitors.

Chapter 7:
Managing Aggressive Competitors

Do you know the saying, "A good offense is the best defense"? It certainly applies when addressing aggressive competitors. Having the skills to manage these competitors will aid you in increasing price effectively and avoiding excessive discounting.

✗ BEST PRACTICE BEHAVIOR GUIDELINES: Defensive Moves

There are two crucial defensive moves to focus on from the disciplined pricing behavior guidelines:

1. React to competitive threats.

2. Return to purposeful behavior.

German Poet, Heinrich Heine wrote, *"We should forgive our enemies, but not before they are hanged."* When it comes to managing aggressive competitors, the quote could read, *"We should forgive our aggressive competitors, but not before we retaliate."*

Reacting to Competitive Threats

If a competitor targets your customers with low price, you can't sit idly by. If there is no negative consequence for this behavior, and they get the occasional positive reinforcement by gaining share, the competitor will continue this action. In fact, they will view it as a winning strategy. They will get bolder and bolder, disrupting the market price. I have watched far too many businesses take this 'do nothing' approach, all with good intentions. They want to model the disciplined behavior they hope to see in others, so they turn the other cheek. While this might be noble, it is a fumble in the pricing world. You can't have competitors believing there are no consequences for going after your accounts. You want them to perceive a cause and effect relationship.

You need to retaliate in a thoughtful manner. While ignoring these competitors is a fumble, there can be fumbles in taking the wrong action. Your retaliatory response must be done in a way that allows the competitor to see a cause and effect rising from their own actions yet also doesn't escalate into a price war.

Case Study 7.1:

A large commoditized product line in DuPont had a disciplined market for many years. Prices had been steadily rising. Then the 2009 recession hit and demand dropped off. A large competitor, or at least one of this competitor's rogue salesmen, decided to use price aggressively against us to gain share. This was mistake number one. Mistake number two was targeting one of DuPont's large, long-time loyal customers. He offered this customer a very attractive price–far below our own price. Not surprisingly, our loyal customer immediately called us. They suggested we would need to match this competitive bid to remain their supplier. Our salesperson quickly huddled with senior sales leadership to decide a response. If we matched this competitor, we would take a large financial hit just at the time our profits were already suffering due to the recession. The leadership decided the best game plan was an 'eye for an eye'.

Within 24 hours, we had a salesperson go into one of the competitor's large and loyal customers. The salesperson talked about our value and why we deserved our fair price. During the discussion, he mentioned that he suspected the customer had much lower prices than our DuPont price since their primary supplier was currently offering new customers prices far below our price. He talked up why DuPont deserved our much higher price. DuPont's assumption going into this negotiation was (1) this customer was likely getting much higher price from his supplier than the 'low ball' offer made to our customer, and (2) this customer likely had no idea that their favorite supplier was offering others much more favorable prices. We will never know if these assumptions were correct, but what followed led us to believe we had guessed correctly.

The very next day, DuPont got a call from our loyal customer. The customer let us know that the 'low ball competitive price' had been pulled off the table—we no longer had to meet it. Thank goodness for an honest customer; that's the reward that comes with loyalty. We surmised that the competitor's loyal customer immediately called their supplier as the DuPont salesperson was exiting the building. This loyal customer likely demanded the same low price they were offering to others. This was a large negative consequence for this competitor. Rather than compound their earlier mistakes, they rescinded their low ball offering to our customer. The trust they had established with their customer over years had been destroyed in one thoughtless move. This company seemed to learn its lesson because we saw no further signs they were targeting our customers with low price.

Let's dissect this case study for the critical elements of success. First, the speed at which we retaliated along with the mention of the same 'low ball price' enhanced the likelihood the competitor would perceive the cause and effect of their own action. They realized that their action had this immediate reaction. Had we waited a week or a month, or even after they had done this to many of our customers, the competitor might not have seen the cause and effect. They might have mistakenly assumed there was no correlation between their actions and our actions. They might have further assumed we were the price aggressive player in the market. Secondly, we didn't over react or react in a punitive way. This competitor targeted one of our accounts and we targeted only one of theirs. Lastly, we made the low-ball price transparent; thus, raising the odds that if the competitor got wind of our actions and heard their low-ball price was raised, the odds of them seeing the connection to their actions increased.

Consider these approaches when dealing with aggressive competitors:

Tactic 1: Go to a few of their best customers. Say something like, *"I understand you are likely getting the very low price of ___ from your current supplier since that is what they are offering other customers, but here is why our offering is higher..."*

Tactic 2: Go to several of their best customers. Offer the exact price you believe they have offered your customers.

Tactic 3: If the competitor appears to be acting on a broad-based strategy of going after your business with price, identify a segment or region of the market where this competitor has a large share and you have a small share. Begin offering low price in this segment. This will have a large negative effect on the competitor and a relatively small negative effect on you. As an example, perhaps you have a large share in the electronics market but little share in the cosmetic market that is dominated by this competitor. Take the price retaliation to the cosmetic customers.

Tactic 4: If this is a new pop-up competitor—one that is small and unlikely to ever amount to a real threat—ignore them. Don't let them distract you from getting your fair price or raising price when the potential volume lose is small.

I prefer tactic 1 over tactic 2. You get your point across without having to compromise your value pricing. As you select the competitor's customer to target, select either a customer in the same territory as your targeted customer and/or select a very large customer. This increases the odds that the competitor's salesperson or business will see the connection. If they target a large customer of yours on the east coast and you retaliate by going to one of their medium-sized accounts on the west coast, they may never see the pattern.

Return to Being Purposeful

Once you have made your point, return to purposeful behavior. Don't continue to go after the competitor's customers with low price. If you do, you will force the competitor to continue with their low-price strategy. You will both lose. Only go to as few customers (maybe only one) as needed to make your point.

If after returning to purposeful behavior, the competitor continues to target your accounts with low price, repeat the process. Retaliate followed by purposeful behavior.

Matching a Competitive Bid

Sales are often faced with the decision to match a competitive bid or not. This framework will help you make a smart decision:

1. Understand the competitor's motivation and offering details.

2. Test the financial impact of your price response.

3. Estimate your potential volume at risk.

4. Consider non-price or alternative price moves.

Step 1. Understand the competitor's motivation and offering details: The first thing you need to do is figure out if this is a one-off move by the competitor's salesperson (as many of these cases are) or if this is a strategic move by the competitor. By strategic move, I mean the competitor set a strategy to go after certain market segments with a low price/gain share strategy. To determine if this is a strategic move or not, look at comparable bids by volume and segment. If this is the rare low-priced bid in this segment, assume you are dealing with a lone wolf salesperson. If you see a pattern of low-priced bids, it's likely a strategic move by the competitor—your business has a little more work to do.

Competitor Low-Price Strategy for Share Gain: Your product line, marketing and/or sales leader should evaluate why they may be making this move then thoughtfully set a strategy to counter (or ignore) this move.

- What is their strategy? What market share do they have today? Which segments are they targeting? Will their business model or value proposition allow them to win?

- What are their weaknesses? What is their reputation? What is their cost, capacity, and profit position?

- Given your assumptions, should you be worried? What strengths does your company offer that can be used to counter this move? Should you use Tactic 3 to retaliate?

Understanding the Competitive Offer: If you are asked to match a competitive bid, uncover the details of that offer to respond effectively. Ask the customer to show you the competitive offer. Legally, he can show this to you since he is asking you to match it. He may elect to 'black out' the suppliers name or other sensitive information beyond the specific offer details. If he is unwilling to show you the details, this is a red flag. Ask him to put the complete competitive bid details (e.g., price, volume, terms, etc.) into an email for you. If this is also refused, the red flag just got bigger. *Is the low-priced competitive bid really a valid offer or is the buyer playing a game?* If they will not share the offer, then ask questions to understand the details—probe deeply. The buyer is likely to only share the information that is in his favor unless you ask direct questions. Consider asking these questions and watch closely for misleading or vague answers:

- *How much volume is offered at this price?*

- *What are the terms and conditions?*

- *Are any services included?*

- *What is the order size or package size? (e.g., is this for full truck load only? for very large order size quantities only?)*

- *What is the lead-time? Are there upcharges for short lead-time deliveries?*

- *What is the product quality?*

- *What is the origin of the material? (e.g., is it coming from overseas?)*

Once you know the detailed offering, determine whether your offering has higher value to this customer in product features, brand/reputation, reliability, and/or the customer experience. If your value is higher, you deserve a premium over the competitive offer, even if you have to provide some price relief. Being the incumbent supplier gives you an additional edge; it is less risk and less hassle for the customer to remain with you. This alone might allow for a slight premium price.

Step 2. Test the Financial Impact of Your Price Response: *Will you have higher profits if you drop price and retain your full volume or are you better to hold your price and accept some volume loss?* This type of price/volume trade-off decision is a *reactive* decision. The calculation for a reactive decision is different than the proactive decision discussed in Chapter 2. (See Table 7.1 for the Reactive Price/Volume Break-even Table.)

REACTIVE PRICE/VOLUME TRADE-OFF DECISION DEFINED

A reactive decision is one made in response to a competitive situation such as responding to a low-priced competitor bid. The price/volume trade-off calculation determines the point where the profit loss from the drop in price or from the loss in volume if you elect not to drop your price are equal. The break-even volume % = % drop in price / % contribution margin.

✂ **Table 7.1.** Reactive Price/Volume Break-Even Table

BREAK-EVEN VOLUME FOR PRICE CHANGE	**Reactive Break-Even Volume Look Up Table** Max. Volume Loss before Matching Competitive Price is Justified			
	Price Decrease In Response to Competitive Price			
Contribution Margin	-2%	-5%	-10%	-20%
10%	20%	50%	100%	200%
15%	13%	33%	67%	133%
20%	10%	25%	50%	100%
25%	8%	20%	40%	80%
30%	7%	17%	33%	67%
35%	6%	14%	29%	57%
40%	5%	13%	25%	50%
45%	4%	11%	22%	44%
50%	4%	10%	20%	40%
55%	4%	9%	18%	36%
60%	3%	8%	17%	33%
65%	3%	8%	15%	31%
70%	3%	7%	14%	29%
75%	3%	7%	13%	27%

Reactive Break-Even Volume = (% Price Change)/ (% Variable Contribution Margin)

Let's explore an example: Your customer has just informed you that a competitor has offered them a price 10% below your price. They have asked you to match this price. The product has a 30% contribution margin. *What volume loss would be the break-even volume (the point at which you should be indifferent between losing the volume or matching the price)?*

From Table 7.1, the break-even volume is 33%. If you believe that you will lose more than 33% of this account, you should consider dropping price. However, if you expect to only lose 20%–25% of this account, your earnings would be higher if you did not respond with a full 10% price drop.

Step 3. Estimate your potential volume at risk: Estimate how much volume you are likely to lose if you don't respond with a price drop. For some it may be the full account, but for most B2B companies it is more likely to be a partial loss of the account. You might have 80% share of the account today and risk being dropped to 60% share (a 25% loss of your volume). Compare this potential volume loss to the break-even volume. If your potential loss is higher than the break-even volume, then you should consider a price concession. On the other hand, if the potential loss is less than the break-even volume you will not match the customer requested price drop. At this point, you can choose to hold your price, consider partial drops, or other alternative moves.

VOLUME ASSESSMENT RISK TIPS

Tip #1: Think through which competitor is likely to pick up your share. Do they really have the additional volume to do this? If so, can they do it quickly, with good reliability, and over the long term? If not, the threat of losing volume might not be as great as the buyer has left you believing.

Tip #2: If you are one of just a few large suppliers, the buyer will likely be reluctant to shift share away from you. Share shifts in a consolidated industry send signals to suppliers that buyers would prefer to avoid. They know if they shift share, the supplier who is awarded this extra volume may well infer they have been underpricing and should raise their price at the next opportunity. Additionally, these buyers don't want to do anything that signifi-

> cantly hurts one of the few large suppliers.
> They know that if one exits the market, their
> prices will go up.

Step 4. Consider partial price or non-price alternative moves: If you have determined you must respond to protect your share, consider partial price drops or even non-price alternative moves to minimize your profit loss *as well as* mitigate future customer price aggression.

Examples of these moves include ensuring you include 'gives or takes' in your response, allowing some premium for your extra value or being the incumbent, and playing on the fears of the buyer should they elect to fully shift away from you as a supplier. Chapter 9 contains extensive guidance on how to effectively drop price including fourteen partial price or non-price alternative tactics.

The next case studies are excellent examples of when walking away or taking a partial price drop are better decisions than meeting a competitive bid.

Case Study 7.2:

A food service distributor, who sold to resellers which in turn sold to the food industry, was faced with a low-priced competitive bid situation. The distributor sold many products to this reseller. The reseller had found an alternative supplier for one of the plastic container products, being imported in from China at roughly 15% lower price. The buyer asked the distributor to match the price to retain the business. The distributor decided to walk away from this container product rather than drop price that low. He knew his value was higher from his quality, his service, his short-lead-time, and his reliability. He also knew, that at a 15% price drop, his profits would be low—too low to risk teaching this reseller that he would drop price on any product just to match the price of an inferior offering. He was not about to risk the supplier proactively finding inferior alternatives for his other products just to leverage his price down. A few months later, the buyer called back wanting to repurchase this product at the distributor's fair price. The buyer was not willing to say why he had changed his mind to buying on value rather than price, yet the distributor eventually learned the reason from the owner of the reseller. Apparently, one of reseller's large restaurant and catering customers was using this imported product at a large event. During the event, they realized the container lids didn't correctly fit the containers—creating a significant problem. This customer called the reseller with the message, "If you ever send me any products from this manufacturer again, I will never do business with you again."

Case Study 7.3:

This large DuPont business, which did a significant portion of their business through a national distributor, faced low-priced imported products in their west coast market. Rather than drop our price across the board to this national distributor, we agreed to drop the price commensurate with the percent of product requiring discounts in the west coast (for example, assume the west coast was 10% of our U.S. market and it required a 10% price drop to defend our share then the U.S. price to the distributor was dropped 1%). This allowed the distributor to be competitive in the west coast while paying DuPont a fair price in the rest of the states. By the following year, the competitor, who was having no success penetrating the west coast, stopped their low-priced imports. As they did, DuPont stopped the price relief to the distributor.

Low-Priced Internet Competitors

It seems like new competitors are popping up on the internet daily. Their value is quite limited—they offer undifferentiated products with no service and often no track record of being a reliable supplier. They must offer low price to compete and they don't seem afraid to offer disruptively low prices.

If customers threaten to shift to these low-priced alternatives unless you match their low prices, consider actions such as:

- Walk away from this business if the volume loss is relatively small (either because the competitor is too small to take much business away or they are not a credible supplier). There is a reasonable chance lost customers will come back to you once they experience the lower-value offering. It may take a few months or until they have an emergency that the new supplier can't handle.

- Let the customer know if they have a problem with their new supplier, you'd be happy to supply them, but it will be as a 'spot customer'. The price will be higher, the services will be removed, the sales relationship will be severely reduced, and lead-times for these unplanned purchases may be longer.

- If you do offer some discount, never match the low-priced option unless the competitive offering truly has the same value in product, customer experience, reliability and brand/reputation—which they rarely do.

- Follow the best practices for identifying the type of buyer you are working with, so you know when the threat to leave you is valid and not just a buyer tactic.

- Review the pricing strategies suggested in Chapter 3 if your business has an online channel.

- Assess your customer vulnerability using the Customer Attractiveness Framework.

Customer Attractiveness Framework

If low-priced suppliers continue to be a problem, it is imperative to understand your customer attractiveness—which customers are most *attracted* to your business and which customers are most *attractive* to your business. Figures 7.1 and 7.2 illustrate a customer attractiveness matrix—both customer mapping and policies. This approach can be valuable in guiding differentiated price and volume strategies and tactics. Examples include:

- Highlights customers or customer groups where you are most vulnerable to price or volume erosion so you can take actions to mitigate risks with your most attractive customers (quadrant B).

- Guides customer mix enrichment.

- Focuses your growth efforts on customers most likely to be good long-term fits (quadrant A).

- Guides policies and tactics for each quadrant to strengthen your profitability (quadrant C and D).

✂ Figure 7.1. Customer Attractiveness Matrix: Customer Mapping

CUSTOMER ATTRACTIVENESS (Revenue, Margin, & Strategic Fit)	B. DEFEND	A. DEFEND & SELECTIVELY GROW
High	• Lee Industries • Distributor B • • • •	• ACME Products • Jones Inc. • Smith LLC • Best Polymers • •
	D. SELECTIVELY REPLACE	**C. CAPTURE MORE VALUE**
Low	• Johnson Inc. • Lee Products • Jurgen Plastics • • •	• Bob's Shop • Hanson LLC • • • •
	We are DISADVANTGAED	We are ADVANTAGED

✂ Figure 7.2. Customer Attractiveness Matrix: Policies

CUSTOMER ATTRACTIVENESS (Revenue, Margin, Strategic Fit)	B. DEFEND	A. DEFEND & SELECTIVELY GROW
High	• Lock in with contracts • Quick fix's to value gaps • Modify offer/price if needed • Meet competitive prices • Communicate your benefits • Strengthen relationships	• Cautiously & selectively grow share • Offer cumulative volume rebates to grow • Adjust offering to evolving needs • Communicate benefits in price increases • Offer temporary price concessions, if needed, linked to long-term relationship / contracts
	D. SELECTIVELY REPLACE	**C. CAPTURE MORE VALUE**
Low	• Raise price or lower cost-to-serve • Walk away if consistently low priced • Price up selectively to exert upward price pressure in market • Test new pricing structures • Add surcharges for services & extras • Don't commit volume / Add price openers	• Communicate value & raise price • Selectively grow share if good price • Cautiously replace accounts that are underpriced given our value • Eliminate low-value, high cost services • Add surcharges on high cost to serve items • Don't commit volume / Add price openers
	We are DISADVANTGAED	We are ADVANTAGED

This framework has four steps.

Step 1. Identify Attractiveness Attributes: Identify attributes that make you more attractive or less attractive to your customer base. Figure 7.3 illustrates this step which will form the basis of your matrix's X axis.

Step 2. Set Customer Criteria: Set your criteria for determining which customers are attractive to your business. Attractive customers should be large customers with decent price and mid-sized customers with good prices. Large customers with low price should not make the cut-off. There may be a few accounts that don't fit these criteria yet get elevated to this status due to strategic fit (e.g., key global accounts, accounts with very large near-term growth expected). This step forms the Y axis of your matrix.

Step 3. Customer Mapping: Map each customer into one of the four quadrants based on the criteria established in step 1 and 2.

Step 4. Set Policies: Determine your policies and tactics for each quadrant. Refer to the example in Figure 7.2 which can be used as a starting point. Adjust it for your business.

Figure 7.3. Customer Attractiveness Matrix: Attractiveness Attributes

OUR VALUE TO CUSTOMER GROUPS	
We are DISADVANTGAED	**We are ADVANTAGED**
• Price buyers • Located next to Competitor A • Don't need application development	• Value our customer experience • Need our unique products • Value our application development • Value our higher reliability • In close proximity to our warehouse • Value our shorter lead-time • Value our global presence

This matrix can be done by each salesperson for their territory, yet it is most powerful when done collectively with your sales team, marketing, and commercial leaders. It not only guides sales but should guide marketing, technology, and leadership as they set short to long-term improvement strategies.

Now that you have your blocking and tackling skills honed, let's work on the skills needed under unfavorable market conditions.

Chapter 8:
Managing through Unfavorable
Market Conditions

It would be wonderful if market conditions were always favorable for higher prices, but that is not likely to be your reality. Many products go through cyclical times—several years of favorable conditions, followed by a few years of weaker market conditions. You need to be prepared for these tough times.

Let's examine the flip-side of favorable market conditions.

- **Loose supply/demand:** When supply and demand becomes loose across an industry, many competitors start to worry and will lower their price to either keep their manufacturing sites operating at a high rate or to offset potential volume loss. They unintentionally start the market price decline. In fact, some suppliers may even begin to drop price in anticipation of a loose market. For example, if they know they are bringing on new capacity in three to six months, they may drop price to tie up higher volume contracts ahead of the new capacity coming on-line.

- **Lower costs:** If your industry's costs decline, your customer may push you to pass along a portion of this decline. The same customer pressures may occur if oil or natural gas prices drop, and they perceive these costs as likely to affect your feedstocks. Customers often have a good rationale for expecting a price decrease—fairness.

If you have been raising your price as your industry's costs increased, fairness would dictate giving some of this back when costs decrease.

- **Competitor decreases:** If your competitors begin decreasing price, you may be forced to follow to protect your share.

- **Brand/value differentiation:** If your brand or offering value has eroded, relative to the competitor's offering or a competitor brings out a new higher value product, your offering may find its price is too high for its relative value.

Additionally, the following situations, while not reasons to drop price, can turn unfavorable dynamics even more unfavorable:

- **Declining market / unfavorable macro-economics or exchange rate:** Declining markets, recessions, and unfavorable exchange rates can all put downward price pressure in the market.

- **Low entry barriers/switching costs:** When new competitors can easily get into the business and/or customers can easily switch between suppliers, you lose some of your pricing power.

- **High-cost percentage of customer's cost:** When your product is a large cost relative to the customer's overall costs they are often quite price sensitive. This is especially true if they can't pass along high costs to their own customer base.

- **Not-in-kind product ceiling:** While you are generally competing against the same product (i.e., an in-kind product), there are times the customer has not-in-kind alternatives. If you are selling a plastic, they may be able to switch to wood or metal. At other times, the alternative is to 'do it themselves' or 'do nothing.' If your price gets too high, suddenly these alternatives become attractive and the customer may switch away from you and your competitors. Understanding this ceiling price can prevent you from inadvertently hurting your overall market size.

The overriding principle, even in unfavorable markets, is to continue to be viewed as fair and trustworthy. At times, that means you might have to drop price across your customer base. The skill comes into play on the way you do the price drop. Your goal is to both delay the decline and minimize the depth of the decline while your customer base pushes for faster, deeper declines.

Unfavorable Market Condition Strategy Framework

Responding to unfavorable conditions should be a strategic decision. It should not be left in the hands of each individual salesperson. Discounting decisions made by individual salespeople, without leadership strategic guidance, can start the price decline for the industry, whether you strategically wanted this to happen or not.

The strategic decision framework is similar to the framework used in favorable conditions. It involves three steps:

1. Analyze the business and industry.

2. Set your strategic pricing plan.

3. Communicate internally and externally.

Step 1. Analyze the Business and Industry: Analyze your business and the industry looking for any rationale that supports holding your price, delaying price drops, or only giving partial price drops. Consider analyzing these areas:

- *Price, Cost, Margin Trends, and their Projection:* Have your costs been increasing or your margin decreasing? Has your price been flat to declining? Is this unfavorable condition projected to be only a few months?

- *Historical Price Increase Practices:* What was the rationale for your past price increases (e.g., rising cost, tight market…)? How fast and effectively did you implement your price increases? Did your past increases have additional rationale beyond this unfavorable condition such as a value-based adjustment or tight supply/demand? Did you do an annual price increase this year? If not, could this be considered a first step in 'giving back price'?

- *By-product and Segment:* What products are materially affected by this unfavorable condition? Are they affected equally? What customers are affected and did these customers fully accept your past increases? Are their current prices at a reasonable level?

- *Market Dynamics:* Are there any favorable market conditions that might offset or trump this unfavorable dynamic? Are your competitors disciplined or aggressive?

- *Competitive Costs:* Are your competitors' products more or less affected than you? Are they likely to act the same as you or differently?

- *Import and Export:* Are different regions of the world affected differently? Does this impact the import and export of products?

Step 2. Set your Strategic Pricing Plan: Rather than dropping price right away, consider holding price, partially dropping, and/or delaying price relief when the following conditions exist for you or your industry:

Your Situation: Your costs are not dropping, previous increases based on rising costs had long delays from when you received the cost increases, some customers didn't fully accept past increases, and/or you eliminated this year's annual increase as a correction for the unfavorable condition

Industry Situation: The industry has tight supply/demand, is not earning the return on investment, and/or has declining margins. Competitors are not, or are less, affected by this unfavorable condition.

Your strategic actions might include some of these following options.

Partial-Drop Strategies:

- Consider a partial drop if you eliminated or reduced your typical annual increase. Credit yourself that amount.

- Credit yourself for portions of past increases that were justified due to reasons beyond just this unfavorable condition. For example, if you had increased price 10% over the past due to a combination of cost increases and value pricing, then consider only dropping price 3%–5% when your costs drop.

- Consider a partial drop if declining material costs are projected to rise again in the next three to nine months.

Delayed Price-Drop Strategies:

- Delay the price decrease for at least as long as you took to raise your price during past favorable conditions.

- Delay the decrease to compensate for margin erosion or very low industry profitability over the past few years.

Selective and Granular Decrease Strategies:

- Only decrease on products materially affected by this unfavorable condition.

- Don't decrease equally across all products if they are not all affected equally.

- Set the specific decrease customer-by-customer contingent upon their historical acceptance of price increases and where their current price is today versus similar sized accounts.

Temporary-Decrease Strategies: If projections or expectations indicate the unfavorable condition might be of short duration, three to nine months, then consider the following:

- Provide 90-day price relief on select products. If the unfavorable condition continues, you can opt to extend the price relief another 90 days.

- Have the price automatically revert to your current price unless you formally extend it.

Step 3. Communicate Internally and Externally: Communicating is as important in a price drop situation as a price increase situation. You want all players in the market to understand your intent and rationale. This engenders the fairness and trust you have been cultivating. It improves the odds that your competitors, faced with similar dynamics, don't take a much more aggressive approach to dropping price.

Once again, the first player to communicate sets the stage for the rest of the industry. So unless you expect your competition to delay more than you delay or drop to a lesser amount, it behooves you to communicate early. For more guidance on communications, refer back to Chapter 4.

Case Study 8.1:

A large business was severely affected by the 2009 recession. The total market demand was down almost 40% in the first quarter of 2009. The world was a far different place than the previous three to four years when the business had increased price two to four times each year based on rising costs, tight market, and value-based adjustments. Customers were pushing hard for price relief. They were well aware that raw material costs for their suppliers were declining. They wanted that reduction passed along to them and they wanted it now.

The business knew that giving price relief was the fair thing to do and that competition was likely to fold under the constant price pressure from the customer base. In the 1st quarter of the year, they analyzed the situation, set their strategic plan, and communicated the points listed below to their customers:

- *Raw materials have dropped and we will be passing along price relief to our customers. This relief will come in the second quarter. When we increased price in the past, due to our raw materials rising, we took months to pass along these increases to you.*

- *Our price drops will be on products A, B, and C; as these are the products materially affected by our lower priced raw materials.*

- *Our price decline will be in the 3%–5 % range depending on the product. Our increases over the past few years have been based on a combination of reasons going well beyond raw material increases. Some increases were based on value and others on basic inflationary costs that are not eroding.*

An additional point was also shared internally and with the specific customers affected:

- *Some customers will receive less price relief than the stated 3%–5% if they had not fully accepted our price increases in the past or their price is noticeably below target.*

We have worked on many of the skills needed to make smart price-drop decisions. It is now time to tie them altogether so you can make smart, easy, effective price-drop decisions every time.

Chapter 9:
Making Smart Price-Drop Decisions

There are four main reasons why customers push back on price:

- **Fairness in Your Rationale:** They don't understand your value or they don't understand the reason for your price increase. Without good understanding, they question the fairness of your price.

- **Fairness versus Other Customers:** They may feel your price is fair, but if they worry that you are giving better prices to other customers they will not feel fairly treated.

- **Tactic, Tactic, Tactic:** Buyers push back on price as a key tactic to test your conviction and your confidence. It allows them to see whether you appear to believe in the fairness of your own price.

- **Fairness in Your Value:** In their eyes, your price is too high given their alternatives. Either they don't value your features or they don't believe those features are worth what you are charging.

If you believe in the fairness of your price, then confidence, conviction, and good communications convince the buyer he is fairly treated. Of the four reasons listed above, only one is a valid reason to drop price—fairness in your value. If your product is not priced correctly, you need to correct the price or offer a lower-value, lower-priced option.

The difficulty in making a price-drop decision is determining whether your price is truly too high or if your price is right. *Is the push back just a tactic?* In general, I found it to be an 90/10 rule. Ninety percent of the time your price is right although you might have to work on your communication of value and fairness. Ten percent of the time, your price may be out of line.

When weak market conditions exist, the smartest move you can make might be to drop price. You are now on the defensive team. A skilled pricing organization must be capable of decreasing as well as increasing price effectively. The fundamentals of pricing (i.e., four market forces, disciplined pricing behaviors, buyer types, etcetera) hold whether you're increasing or decreasing price. You ask essentially the same questions. When the responses indicate favorable dynamics for you and high pricing power for you, you hold or raise price. When the responses indicate unfavorable dynamics for you and low-pricing power for you, you consider dropping price.

Your three main goals, relative to smart price drop decisions are to:

- reduce your price only as low as necessary,
- gain something of value or take something away for giving up price, and
- delay the price reduction for as long as you can appropriately do so.

The following checklist and guidance will help you manage all three.

⚒ Price-Drop Decision Checklist

When considering a price drop, answer the following questions which are illustrated in Figure 9.1. If most answers are in the "favorable to drop," category then move forward with a decrease. Likewise, if most answers are "unfavorable to drop," rethink the need to drop your price. Unfortunately, it is not quite as simple as adding up the number of responses in each category and siding with the highest responses. If one category does not dominate, then you will have to use your newly learned skills and judgement to determine your action.[i]

Figure 9.1. Price-Drop Decision Guideline

		Favorable to drop ✚	Unfavorable to Drop ▬
All Situations	1. Why?	Competitive threat	Customer request / share gain
	2. Consequence of not dropping?	Big share lost	No / little share lose
	3. Which competitor?	Large / reliable	New / small / not local
	4. Customer's buying behavior?	Price buyer	Loyal
	5. Product differentiation	Commodity	Unique
	6. Customer needs changing?	Lower needs	The same / higher
	7. Relative account price / margin?	High	Same / low
Situational	8. Break-even price/volume trade-off?	Volume lose hurts profits	Price lose hurts profits
	9. Competitive reaction?	Will not know or react	Will know / Will react
	10. Competitive offering?	Better	Same / Worse
	11. Market fairness?	Loose market / dropping costs	Tight market / rising costs

1. Why are you considering a drop?

Favorable to drop: Competitors are lowering prices or to stimulate increased market size

Unfavorable: To meet customer desire/expectation, to gain share or to pull sales forward into the next financial quarter/year

2. What will happen if you don't drop price?

Favorable to drop: Likely large share loss

Unfavorable: No or small share loss

---

[i] *A simple excel tool that streamlines this content as well as calculates the price decision is available through www.price2profits.com*

3. **To whom will you lose the share?**

   Favorable to drop: One of the top suppliers

   Unfavorable: A new, small, or low-end competitor or an opportunistic importer

4. **What is the customer's traditional buying behavior?**

   Favorable to drop: A price buyer—not loyal, switches suppliers often

   Unfavorable: Loyal relationship or value buyer to you or to one of your competitors

5. **Is your product differentiated?**

   Favorable to drop: Undifferentiated or commodity products

   Unfavorable: Slightly to very unique products

6. **Are customer needs changing? Is your value proposition clear?**

   Favorable to drop: Competitors are closing the gap, the customer no longer needs your value

   Unfavorable: Your value is clear and the customer needs this value.

7. **What is the account variable margin?**

   Favorable to drop: High or higher than similar customers

   Unfavorable: The same or lower than similar customers

8. **What is the break-even volume?**

   Favorable to drop: Contribution dollars increase. Profits from the volume gain (or sustain) more than offset the profit loss from dropping the price.

Unfavorable: Contribution dollars from volume gain (or sustain) will not offset the profit loss from price decline. Total profitability will decline.

9. **Will there be a competitive reaction or spillover to other customers?**

    Favorable to drop: Competitors and other customers are unlikely to know of your price drop, so no spillover effect is expected. Competitors are unlikely to drop price even if they know.

    Unfavorable: Your price drop is likely visible to competitors and/or other customers. Spillover is likely. Competitors will probably react with even further price drops.

Question ten applies if you have a direct competitive threat and question eleven is only relevant for unfavorable market dynamics.

10. **What is the competitive offering, including value, terms, volume, etc. compared to your offering?**

    Favorable to drop: Comparable to or better than yours. Competitor is a large, reliable supplier with a sustainable offer.

    Unfavorable: Lower value offering. Competitor is an untried or potentially unreliable supplier. Competitor is only offering a one-time buy or a short-term offer. Buyer is unwilling to show you, or provide details of, the competitive bid he/she has asked you to match.

11. **Do you have a solid rationale for holding/increasing price given these market conditions? How did you justify increases in the past?**

    Favorable to drop: No solid rationale for holding/increasing price. Past increases were done based on your rising raw material costs which are now dropping. The customer volume is increasing significantly.

Unfavorable: There is a solid rationale for holding/increasing price. Customer is below average on profitability. Customer volume is dropping. Your raw material costs are increasing. Your offering has higher value than that of competitors.

Skill Drill:

Your Challenge: You are considering a 10% price drop for one of your large customers—they have indicated they may consider other suppliers if you don't reduce your price. Your relationship with this customer has always been good. They are a relationship buyer and you think the worst case scenario is a loss of 20%–25% share. Your assessment of the situation is shown in Figure 9.2. *Will you drop price or hold?*

Figure 9.2. Price-Drop Decision Example Assessment

		Favorable to drop ➕	Unfavorable to Drop ▬
All Situations	1. Why?	Competitive threat	√ Customer request
	2. Consequence of not dropping?	Big share lost	√ No / little share lose
	3. Which competitor?	√ Large / reliable	New / small / not local
	4. Customer's buying behavior?	Price buyer	√ Loyal
	5. Product differentiation	√ Commodity	Unique
	6. Customer needs changing?	Lower needs	√ The same / higher
	7. Relative account price / margin?	High	√ Same / low
	8. Break-even price/volume trade-off?	Volume lose hurts profits	√ Price lose hurts profits
Situational	9. Competitive reaction?	√ Will not know or react	Will know / Will react
	10. Competitive offering?	Better	√ Same / Worse
	11. Market fairness?	Loose market / dropping costs	Tight market / rising costs

Analysis: If you decided not to drop price, you are correct. Not only are more of the answers in the "unfavorable to drop" category, but the fact that this is a loyal customer should further reinforce your confidence in your pricing power. However, you should be concerned that this loyal customer might not be feeling fairly treated; thus, you should reinforce to the customer your value, the fairness of the price, and their importance to your company.

⚒ Guidance on How to Effectively Drop Price

If it looks like dropping price might be the smart move, first consider these preemptive moves before the price-drop options that follow:

- Go beyond the buyer and reach out to the users of your products or the organization that gets the value from your offer. Play on their fears and uncertainties. Let them know there is a risk, a hassle, or even additional costs in shifting to a new supplier. Recruit these users/value receivers to advocate to their buyer on your behalf.

- If the situation is in response to a low-priced competitor bid, quickly try to retaliate against this competitor (per guidance in Chapter 7) in the hopes of having them stop their aggressive pricing.

- Improve your communications of the value, fairness of your price and the importance of the customer to you.

These suggestions—to minimize the decrease, minimize future customer price aggressiveness, and/or improve the timing—pull together all the price-drop related suggestions mentioned throughout the book.

Tactic 1: Value Pricing: If you have additional value over the competitive offer, don't drop your price as far. Consider only a partial drop. Your customer might be asking for a 10% drop, but you may counter with a 5% or 6% drop, given your value.

- Consider all elements of product, quality, service, brand, reliability, and relationship value.
- Consider factors such as switching cost and/or perceived risk of switching.
- Get all the details of the competitive offer you're being asked to match.

Tactic 2: Take Something Away: If you must drop, do so like a value pricer. Take something away.

- Examples: Less services, longer lead times, shorter payment terms, shorter contract commitment, no custom products, no technical support, freight excluded, weekday delivery only, ship to one location only, shift to make-to-order versus off-the-shelf, limit the volume at this lower price

Tactic 3: Get Something of Value: Rather than taking something away as you drop price, you could consider getting something of value for your company.

- Examples: More share or volume, longer contract commitment (if this is an attractive account), first right to bid on their future applications, access to performance data on your products versus competitive products, access to decision makers, a modified formula pricing structure, endorsements or price openers in the contract

Tactic 4: Add More Value: Consider adding value that appeals to the customer rather than dropping price.

- Examples: Additional services, extension of warranties or guarantees, shorter lead times, co-branding, six-month exclusivity on new products, first rights to test your new products, credit, training sessions, financing options

Tactic 5: Temporary, Select, or Delayed Incentives: Instead of giving them a long-term discount, consider time or volume limited options as well as delaying the discount.

- Temporary or Select Examples: Temporary 90-day discount or rebate, 60-day trial period at X% discount, only X tons.
- Delayed Examples: Announce a discount is coming in two months or after X units are bought. Offer a rebate after the customer buys Y units.

Tactic 6: Incumbent Value: If you are the incumbent supplier, this is often worth a slight price premium so customers can avoid the risk and hassles of changing suppliers.

- Examples: Minimum 2%-3% higher than an alternate supplier of like reputation or minimum 5% higher for less established supplier

Tactic 7: Secondary Supplier Position: If you are not the primary supplier, don't be pushed into matching the price of the primary supplier. You should have a higher price since the customer is buying less product from you.

- Example: Price several percent higher if you have noticeably less volume than the primary supplier.

Tactic 8: Bailing Out the Primary Supplier: Assuming you are the secondary supplier, don't bail out the primary supplier or provide all the services for the full account without being rewarded. Limit the customer's use of services (or raise the price) and add monthly volume maximums to your contract. If they need more volume than the monthly volume maximum to bail out the underperforming primary supplier, charge a premium for this additional volume. Let them know that this extra volume is not in your company's supply planning and in order to accommodate their unexpected needs, it requires additional effort and cost in your operations.

- Example: Use a higher price or surcharge for additional services beyond the agreement or significant volume beyond their typical monthly buy (e.g., 10% cap over the typical month or 10% cap versus their forecast).

Tactic 9: Threats to Add a Second Supplier: If the customer threatens to add a second supplier, or just to drop your share by ~20%, consider tactics such as reductions or rebates only on their last increment of purchases or walking away from this volume while raising their price slightly.

- Reduction on last increment of business example: First 100 tons at $2/ton and next 10 tons at $1.90/ton or use cumulative volume rebates.

- Walk Away example: Walk away from this portion of the business but also raise price 2%–3%, based on their lower volume. (The increased price will offset much of the profit loss from the volume decline.)

- End-user customer-specific rebate example: Rebate only on portion of product that your customer sells through to low-value, end-user applications.

Tactic 10: Adjust Rebates or Volume Discounts: If you do end up losing volume, remove or adjust pre-existing volume related rebates or discounts that were based on their larger buy. During the negotiation, let them know this is one of the consequences of lower volume.

- Example: Shift from something like 5% discount from list price to 5% rebate if purchases hit a quarterly minimum of X.

Tactic 11: Consider Offering Two or Three Choices: Offer choices to stimulate value discussions and better meet customer needs. Examples:

- Low value/low price: Core products only, six-weeks lead-time, full truckload and no service
- Mid value/mid-price: Most products, one-week lead time, technical service
- High value/high price: All products, two-day lead time, technical service including a 24-hour hotline

Tactic 12: Discount Less Than Expected in Unfavorable Market Conditions: Example reasons:

- Credit yourself for eliminating this year's annual increase as an adjustment for declining raw materials
- Credit yourself if past increases were only partially due to rising costs—the other portion was due to value price adjustments or tight supply/demand.
- Reduce discounts to customers who didn't fully accept past increases or who have a price below floor price.

Tactic 13: Reduce Price Only on At-risk Products/Markets: Avoid the trap of thinking you need to reduce all your products or across all your markets if the volume risk is isolated to one product or one market segment.

- Examples: 5% on commodity grades ABC; 0% on unique grades DEF

Tactic 14: Switch Products: Encourage customers to switch to a product that's more attractive to you (higher margin, core product). Examples:

- Products A and B are both priced at $2/kg, but product B has 10% higher contribution margin. Lower product B price slightly and shift customer from product A to B.
- Shift away from custom/very low volume products

If you are following this advice, you will be telling customers "no" on their discount requests far more often. You will want to tell them in a way that builds trust and fairness.

It's time to practice conversation skills including telling the customer "No".

Chapter 10:
Price-Pressure Negotiation
Discussions

Salespeople are frequently faced with price pressure. When faced with this pressure, you need to defuse the situation and shift the conversation away from price until you learn more—or teach more. Your primary goal is threefold:

- **Identify the type of buyer; thus, your pricing power:** Are you talking to a true price buyer or is this really a value buyer pretending to be a price buyer? Your pricing power goes up if this buyer cares about something other than price.

- **Bring new insights that generate value beyond price:** Even if the buyer enters the negotiation as a staunch price buyer, providing new insights can possibly switch their view to valuing certain features of your offering.

- **Create a win-win offering:** Find the best offering for the customer, even if that offering is different than initially anticipated by either of you, then get a fair price for this offering.

The conversation should address positive and negative points—the carrot and the stick. Focus on the positive yet subtly introduce the negative implications of reducing your volume.

Positive messages:

- **You are important to us:** We appreciate your business. We value you. We have always had a trusting, respectful relationship. We want that to continue.

- **We are a value pricer:** We price our products based on fair value to our customers. We do not compete on low price. We know the value of our offering and price it fairly.

- **This Price is fair relative to others:** Our price is fair and consistent with the price we offer to similar customers. (When said in reference to a third party the message carries more physiological weight. For example, "Your peers feel our price is fair. They are accepting this price.")

Negative messages:

- **We have better options:** Subtly and cautiously indicate you will look to place this volume with other customers who are willing to pay your fair price if they aren't interested.

- **It is risky for you to walk away:** Play on or build their fears that other competitors offer less value. If they need you as a backup supplier, you might not have available product. If you do, it will be at market or spot purchase price. (Deliver this message to the user in addition to the buyer.)

- **If you lower our volume, our price will increase:** Let them know the price you offered is contingent on a specific volume. If they opt to lower your volume, the price will increase to the appropriate level for that volume point.

- **If you wait, our price might increase:** Indicate the price you are offering is only guaranteed for a limited time. After that time, a new—possibly higher—price will be quoted.

The customer should sense you are confident and committed to getting a fair price. They should also sense you are in no rush and will not be hurried into a decision.

Let's set the stage. You are talking with a customer about a new deal. You have asked pre-qualifying questions and feel confident you are a viable supplier. Early in the negotiation the customer starts right in on price: "*Your price is too high!*" *or "I only care about the price so, tell me now, what is your price?"*

Follow the framework in Figure 10.1 to smoothly bust through this tough price negotiation.

PRICE PRESSURE NEGOTIATION FRAMEWORK

Figure 10.1. Price Pressure Negotiation Framework

Qualify the Deal				
• Why are you looking to replace your current supplier? • What is the bidding and decision making process, timing & criteria for the deal?				
1. Defuse & Redirect	**2. Uncover Needs; Price & Non-Price**	**3. Share Insights & Solutions**	**4. Test Options & Compare**	**5. Influence & Align**
• I understand price is most important to you. • May I ask a few questions so I can better meet your needs at the lowest fair price?	• What are your product and service needs? • Why are these important to you? • What are you trying to achieve with your lower price request?	• Did you know this problem ____ is widespread in your industry. • Our offering solves this problem saving you $_____.	• Would you be interested if I remove services to get a lower price? If so, can you give me...? • Our offering is 2X as effective as our competitor at only 5% premium.	• We're committed to delivering value and we price for our value. • This is a fair price for this offering. • If only price matters, we might not be your best choice.

Pre-step: Qualify the Deal: If this is a new customer, or even a new product or higher volume with an existing customer, you need to qualify them. *This should be done early in your first conversation so that it precedes the negotiation and the customer turning the discussion to price.* Qualifying a customer means you are testing to determine if you are truly a viable contender to get this business as opposed to being brought in only as a threat to the preferred vendor.

✘ *Buyer Qualification Checklist*: Ask your customer these qualifying questions:

1. ***Current Supplier:*** *Are you already buying a similar product or service? If so, from whom? If not, what are you doing instead?*

2. ***Satisfied:*** *Are you satisfied with your current supplier? Why or why not? If satisfied, why are you considering other suppliers?*

3. ***Decision Maker:*** *Who are the decision makers? When can I speak with them?*

4. ***Bidding Process:*** *What is the process, timeline, and criteria for decisions?*

5. ***Information:*** *When or how do I get information on your needs? What will it take for me to win?*

6. ***Other Suppliers:*** *How many suppliers are bidding? Are any of them preferred? Will you be selecting just one or will you have multiple suppliers?*

If you suspect the buyer is only looking for a low price so they can leverage a lower price from their preferred supplier, don't fall into that trap (refer to Chapter 6 for strategies). Additionally, you should prepare using the *Negotiation Planning Checklist* covered in Chapter 5.

Step 1. Defuse and Redirect: Acknowledge that you understand pricing is very important to them. Let them know that you want to ask a few questions about their needs so you can provide them the offering that best meets these needs given their price concerns. Ask them if they are fine with you asking these questions. Let them know, you will come back to their price concerns with potential solutions after you get further information. Get their okay to hold off on the price discussion for a few minutes. It is critical for you to shift away from price and onto value discussions.

Step 2. Uncover Needs—Price and Non-Price: This is a time to listen and learn; avoid moving quickly to price concessions until you have a deep understanding of their needs.

Stated Needs: Ask deeper questions about their needs. Probe to understand why these needs are important. Ask them to quantify their problems or the benefits to solving them. Pose questions such as: *"How bad is your reactor yield? If you could prevent this yield lost, what is that worth to you?"*

Pricing Needs: Uncover their rationale for why price is so important to them. Don't assume you know the answer to this question. Their response may well help to uncover a need that you can solve in a different way than just low price. Ask them, *"Why is reduced price so important? What are you trying to achieve with this lower price?"*

Unstated Needs: Probe further into any favorable services, payment terms, or value you provide to test the importance of these with this customer.

Step 3. Insights & Solutions: During these discussions one of the most effective ways to close a deal is to challenge the customers with new insights which help the customer with their business success. The Corporate Executive Board has done studies to prove the power of this approach and it is the core principle in the sales effectiveness book, "The Challenger Sale" by Matthew Dixon and Brent Adamson.

Essentially, during the deal setting phase (or for existing customers throughout the relationship) if you teach the customer something of value to their business that they hadn't fully understood, then provide a unique solution to this compelling issue, you raise the odds of making the value sale. If your product helps improve their yield, ask about the value for yield improvement. Say something such as, *"Many of our customers have poor yield in their operations and have seen as much as 20% improvement with our product saving about $100,000 per year for companies your size. Is yield an issue for your operations? Would this benefit be of value to you?"* If part of your value includes providing downstream market insights that help the customer win, then provide insights such as, *"In your industry, many customers value branded products and this can be an opportunity to grow and distinguish yourself from competition by..."*

Explore areas that align with your unique strengths such as the importance of reliability, security of supply, lead-times, quality, relationships, marketing support, lobbying efforts, regulatory support, etcetera. Don't assume the buyer knows all her needs. She may not be aware of certain value you can provide, and thus have not thought about whether this is a need or not.

Step 4. Test and Compare: In this portion of the conversation, you will begin to test your theory of the buyer type, and potential offering/price options. This enables you to help the customer compare your offering/price, as well as its value, to potential competitive offers they may be exploring.

Test Offering Options and Buyer Type: Test if this is a true price buyer, or a value buyer in disguise, by identifying what you believe might be one or two of their biggest needs, then explore offerings that remove these needs to get at lower price. If the buyer insists on having those needs included or insists on comparing the price with or without these needs included, then there is high likelihood this is a value buyer: you have higher pricing power. The conversation might go something like this: "*Would you be interested in offering options that exclude short lead times and technical service if I were able to provide you a lower price?*" You are not necessarily trying to put forward the best offering for them as of yet or even necessarily a real option; you are just trying to test their conviction to '*lowest price is the only thing that matters.*' Once you establish this answer, you are ready to explore real options to find the win-win solution for the customer and you.

Initially, offer options that are at or higher value than the stated needs. In other words, push for the upsell and avoid offering lower value options if they have not clearly indicated a need for these choices. When it is clear that you need to put forward additional options, help them compare the trade-offs between your own offering options: the higher-value and higher-priced offering versus the lower-value and lower- priced option. If you are providing the concession of a lower-value offer, this is an ideal time to ask for a concession from them.

Take the time to prepare your options, especially the price point. Break the negotiation into a second session if you feel that would be beneficial. This break could potentially give you time to talk beyond the buyer to the users who value your offering. Perhaps ask these users to advocate on your behalf.

Compare Your Offering Options and Competitor Offerings: Expand your comparisons to competitors' offerings. This can be a wonderful opportunity to ensure your offering is being considered in its best and accurate light, relative to competitive choices, and to make the buyer's job easier. In some cases, this comparison might be enough to allow the customer to decide on the spot without doing their own due diligence.

The better you can quantify your value in financial terms, and prove your benefits, the more likely you are to get a higher price premium and close the deal. Their perception of the certainty that they will get the stated benefits goes a long way to your success. Include benefit quantification, case studies, endorsements, or other information that influences the perception towards guaranteed benefits.

Step 5. Influence and Align: At this point, you are ready to close the deal. You are essentially aligned on the offering and its value and probably even the price. However, the buyer may make another run at getting some price concession.

The Soft Push: The buyer has turned friendlier and more open to discussion. They inquire if there isn't something else you could do to reduce their price just a little further. They test your conviction and play on your newly developed relationship. This is the time to hold firm—to ensure them this is your fair and appropriate price.

The Hard Push: The buyer may try to delay the decision in the hopes of making you nervous thus undermining your confidence. They may imply they will be exploring other options or they need to get input or approvals from others in the company. From your qualifying questions, you should have a feel for the decision timeline so you can assess if this delay had already been in their plan. Offer to provide more information if needed. Counter their push back by playing on their fears. Use the negative messages listed earlier as a way of letting them know you will need management approval for your offering/price point. A second tactic the buyer might employ is to threaten or proceed with a formal RFQ process. If this is a requirement in their procurement process, one that you can't get around (which you should know from asking your qualifying questions earlier), accept it. However, if you suspect it is not a firm requirement, dissuade them from this approach. Steer the conversation towards a mutually acceptable alternative rather than going through this formal bid process.

✗ Additional Price Negotiation Tips

GENERAL

These general tips, may sound like common sense, but I often see inexperienced salespeople not follow this advice.

- Boldly ask questions about other supplier's bidding on the business and the types of offers they are putting forth, especially if the buyer mentions they have lower priced offers.

- Assess your pricing power—don't assume the customer is a price buyer and thus your power is low.

- In the face of clear evidence that you are dealing with a price buyer don't hold firm on providing a high-value/high-price offer unless it is your intention to walk away from this account. Listen more closely and uncover the true buyer needs, then consider better options.

PREPARATION

Align the Sales Team: For broad-based increases, leadership must prepare the sales team (e.g., the fairness of the increase, talking points, confidence, etc.)

Prepare for or Roll-Play Tough Negotiations: Anticipate the possible arguments and requests that your customers might ask for. Formulate your responses. This will greatly help your confidence and ability to resist price pressure.

Sell Value to Users First: When possible, sell your value to the users or decision makers before selling to the procurement organization. The users or decision makers will provide more information thus allowing you to better quantify your value. They may also provide 'pull' for you with the buyer.

Downstream Pull-through Sales: If your value/benefits are high or higher downstream from your direct customer, consider pull through sales. This works well in industries that sell through distributors to installers. Often the offering value is greatest with the installer; thus, it makes sense to sell at your point of value and let 'pull through' sales work for you. Another example includes pharmaceuticals where reaching out to the patient can create pull through to the doctors.

Multiple Negotiators: For large, tough price buyers, you may benefit from bringing a second negotiator with you. The second person will likely be less emotionally tied to this account and can think more rationally. Collaborating on the negotiation can lead to smarter decisions.

SETTING THE STAGE

Anchoring: Be the first to communicate price targets: go first and go high. This will shape the buyers' perception of value and draws the buyer upward in his pricing expectations. The first party to discuss prices or terms typically has the largest influence on the outcome. This sets the starting point of the negotiation. (Yet avoid shifting the negotiation into a price discussion too early.)

Reference Price: Mention a very high priced related product to subtly influence the buyer to thinking your price is reasonable or quite favorable. You might mention that your raw materials have increased 10% just before letting them know that your price increase is 5%. Or, for example, you may mention specialty polymers sell for $4–$10/lb. but your mid-value polymer is priced at $2/lb.

Lead with High-End Offering: Start negotiations with your higher-end offering or with a product that has all the services bundled in. If the buyer is unwilling to pay for these services, then begin to unbundle and strip down the offering. (It is harder to start with your lowest price offering and then upsell extras.)

Exude Confidence: Demonstrate confidence from your words to your non-verbal actions. Speak as if you know the deal is a done deal.

Speak with Emotion: Research has repeatedly shown that speaking with intensity and emotion is often perceived as more genuine and credible.

Look them in the Eye: Looking another person in the eye or conversely, avoiding eye contact, is a key nonverbal cue on your credibility.

Compliment the Customer: Genuine compliments can help build relationships and disarm the buyer. Just don't overdo it.

NEGOTIATING & CONCESSIONS

Reciprocity Ploys: People feel compelled to make a concession after one has been given to them. So, if the buyer asks for a concession you are willing to give, you can ask for a bigger concession than the concession you gave. They will be inclined to grant it. Additionally, it works if you give a small gift such as a pen or a book upfront. This will lean your buyer towards giving you a concession in return.

Start with Extra Non-essentials: Consider starting the deal with a few non-essential terms or conditions that you can concede without hurting your profitability. These concessions may make the buyer feel they have won something as well as encouraging them to be more open to giving you a concession in return.

Ask for More: If you want something, don't be afraid to ask for it. There is no need to wait for the customer to ask for something first.

Don't Give Just Because They Asked: Many salespeople believe they must give a concession just because the customer asks for one. They feel it will hurt the trusting relationship if they do not respond. This is not necessary. If you have the pricing power, and your price is fair, don't provide the concession. Explain your position and move on.

TIME AND THREATS

Don't Get Rushed into A Decision: The buyer may insist on a lower price and try to rush you into making the decision on the spot. Don't be rushed unless you have envisioned the scenario ahead of time. Being forced into a quick answer is almost always in the favor of the buyer not the seller. If you're their preferred supplier, you will not lose the account because you need time to prepare a proper response. Slow responses often send better non-verbal signals than fast ones. Only in true emergencies do you need to act quickly.

Ignore Threats to Buy Elsewhere: Ignore or downplay threats to buy elsewhere as if they don't worry you. Remain visibly confident in your position. Utilize some of the negative messages listed earlier in this chapter.

Be Ready to Walk Away: Before going into a negotiation, know your walk away position. If you opt to walk away due to an unfair low price, do so in a way that preserves or builds the relationship for potential future deals. Just the act of walking away may well turn the negotiation around. However, if they do shift to another supplier, one of lesser value, there is a good chance they will come back once they experience this lower value option.

INFLUENCING PERCEPTION OF VALUE

Psychology of pricing tactics are often used in business-to-consumer (B2C) sales (e.g., promotions, sale on Wednesday only, or Kohl's $10 cash back for every $50 spent this weekend). Many of these tactics can be used effectively in the B2B world.

Trials and New Customers: Allowing a customer to try your product before buying can be helpful in not just closing the deal but also doing it at higher price. Psychology studies show that people value something more if they own it, even for just a brief time.

Fear of Missing Out: Play on the fear of missing out on a deal by offering restricted deals (e.g., 'only until Friday', 'for the first ten customers', or 'only for the first 100 units').

Stress Your Large Potential Benefits and Low Potential Risk: Many decision makers make their decisions based on the potential value of gains relative to the risks. For example, buying lottery tickets has a small risk yet potentially a big pay out.

Offer Choices: Offering three choices is better than offering two choices. If you offer three choices, such as a low-end, a mid-range, and a high-value brand, a significant percent of people, who would have bought the low-end brand, will shift their buy from the low-end brand to the mid-range brand. This is especially true when the buyer is not intimately familiar with the products or services and their value. Adding the 'high-end' brand makes your main product seem more reasonably priced.

Most Popular, Best Selling, or Best Value Label: If you provide several brands or offering packages, then labeling one of the offerings as best seller, best value, or most popular can shift buyers towards this preferred offering.

Loyalty Programs: Loyalty programs target people's desire to achieve the top goal—to be recognized and rewarded as special. In the roofing industry, roofing material suppliers will certify their top installers and may even have an elite certified status. These roofers market themselves as certified and get access to training and additional services. In return, they need to be loyal to the manufacturer. Another example is when customers buy sufficient quantities to hit your loyalty target to get invitations to special events or access to extras such as training, economist reports, and marketing materials. If there is a threshold for providing this extra attention, be sure the customer knows it so it influences their behavior.

Rebate Voucher or Coupons: Rebate vouchers or coupons that must be used within a short window of time (e.g., 1 week) can be effective largely because many people forget to submit the rebate or use the coupon in the allowed timeframe. Even if the coupon is used, it may draw additional volume to your business. In businesses with storefronts, such as parts and equipment stores geared to installers, periodically giving a coupon "good for next week" with the current purchase can drive repeat business. These tools should not be used too often or too predictably so buyers don't catch on and change their buying behaviors to get all the benefits without the return of the extra volume.

Upsell after the Deal is Done: For price-sensitive buyers, a low-priced offer may be needed to close the deal. Once the deal is done, attempt to upsell them on your additional services or higher-value products.

Quantify Financial Benefits: One of the highest drivers of customer loyalty is providing financial quantification of your value or benefits. This engenders the perception of certainty in the results. People will steer toward a certain positive benefit over a slightly better yet uncertain option.

Use Limited Knowledge with Confidence: It is difficult to state or quantify a customer's expected benefits from your offering when you have limited customer knowledge. Make an educated guess and state it with high confidence. If you are wrong, the buyer is likely to correct you, providing you with valuable information. You might say, *"Most companies like yours have a yield loss of 10%, so presuming you do as well, the benefits to your company are..."*

Put it in Writing: People tend to believe something in writing over something verbal. The perception of truth increases if it comes from a third party. If you have a third party award or recognition (e.g., good housekeeping seal of approval, FDA (Food & Drug Administration approved), show this in your written material or website.

Price/Quality Effect: Price is often perceived as an indicator of quality, especially if the buyer is not knowledgeable about the offering. Think of wine. Most of us expect a $50 bottle of wine to be better than the $20 bottle, which should be better than the $8 bottle. Know your customers; at times raising price might be the better option.

Price Framing: Set your price in a way that makes it appear smaller. For example, if you sell drums of product for $100/drum, you could shift to selling it as $20/lb. For services consider presenting your price as $100/month rather than $1200/year. For equipment, it might be $800 with mail-in rebate rather than saying $1000. You can also frame a discussion to focus on total cost of ownership or value per price rather than straight price.

Exclusivity: Present a deal that has something unique or exclusive for the customer or a specific customer group. This can motivate buyers. Perhaps it is exclusive rights to a new innovative product, for a select group, for one year. Or they are chosen to be in your certified-installer program.

Location Matters: Adjust your price based on your location. People will pay more for a coffee in the airport or a fancy hotel without complaint. B2B Buyers are likely to pay more in cities, or fancier stores/offices.

Quote Others: It is more effective to say that other customers have accepted your price as a fair price, than to say, *"My price is fair."* Likewise, if there is a third-party source of information, beneficial to your negotiation position, or a decision maker/user source you can quote, it is better than stating the same point as your position.

You're almost over the finish line. The next chapter discusses the rare times when actively going for an interception (i.e., dropping price) might be a wise strategy.

Chapter 11: Dropping Price as a Proactive Strategy

Strategically dropping price to grow profits is a risky move that often backfires. Yet there are times when the risk is worth it. The following highlights times where a *business-wide* decision to do this might make sense and over the long-haul improve your profits.

Be the Low-Priced Supplier

Being the low-price supplier can be a successful strategy when you (1) have noticeably lower internal costs than your competition, and (2) the volume share you gain by offering a lower price is significantly greater than the price/volume trade-off break-even point. Since lower-priced business models often have low contribution margins, let's say 20%–30%, that means if you price 10% under your competitors, you will need to pick up well over 50%–100% more volume to make this a winning strategy. Not an easy task. You also need to factor in the competitive reaction and their willingness/ability to drop price near yours to defend their own share. If your competitor's cost position will not allow them to drop anywhere near your prices, and you pick up the game-changing volume, it might be worth considering.

Dropping Price to Encourage Industry Consolidation

When there are many players in the market, and the market is oversupplied, businesses may adopt a strategy of low price in the hopes of encouraging some players to exit the market. If they are successful, a tighter market will allow for higher prices in the future. This risky strategy will result in lower profits for a few years while waiting for someone to exit the market. Leadership needs to be committed to this multiyear strategy including the 'years of reduced profits.'

This strategy is best done when you have a low-cost position in the industry and there are noticeably higher-cost players who would experience negative earnings if the market price drops while you still maintain positive earnings. It often takes a year or more as these high-cost players hope the market price will turn favorable again if they just wait. Furthermore, there are large cost hurdles for shutting down a manufacturing site (severance pay, dismantlement fees, etc.) so weak players may opt to sell their assets to another competitor—one that might be able to run it more profitably. Also, they may mothball the asset so that they could easily bring it back on-line should the market price rise in the future.

Case Study 11.1:

A large chemical industry player enjoyed a low-cost position in a global commoditized market—one that had excess capacity. They assessed which competitors' assets were vulnerable if the market price fell. The business decided to embrace a low-price, share-growth strategy recognizing this would likely start a price war hurting profitability in the short term. They knew they were in for a multiyear strategy; one in which they would remain profitable yet less profitable than they would have with a high-priced strategy. As they implemented their lower price (with a public announcement), they initially picked up a few percent share, but competitors quickly began dropping price to protect their share. It was nearly two years before they began to see the first competitors exiting the market or shutting down higher cost assets. In the end, roughly five manufacturing sites, worldwide, were shutdown. Supply and demand came into balance and eventually got tight. Then they, as well as the other remaining competitors, began increasing price. In the end, they had a far healthier market.

Correcting Your Value Price

Many new products or services begin with unique value over existing alternatives. They deserve to be rewarded and compensated for this innovation—pricing with a premium. Over time, as the offering matures, other competitors generally improve their own offerings to close the value gap. As this happens, a high price premium is no longer warranted. Dropping your target price, to better balance your price with your value relative to competition, is the smart decision. This will avert volume loss.

Likewise, if the customer's need for your value has declined, then it is no longer worth the full price premium to them as it had been.

Declining Industry

If you are in a rapidly declining industry—one that is well over supplied—consider dropping price to be the last man standing. Of course, you must have a good cost position, relative to your competitors, to make this a feasible strategy. The last few players, in a declining market, often enjoy very good prices.

Case Study 11.2:

I worked in a DuPont fluorocarbon business that was undergoing a full product transformation due to environmental issues. Certain products were being phased out through government regulations. Throughout the multiyear transition there were cyclical periods of overcapacity in the market followed by someone shutting down an asset followed by temporary market tightness. Each time the market turned loose, prices would fall until another asset was shut down, then suppliers enjoyed a temporary high-priced market. DuPont was in a favorable position due to multiple assets around the globe and a good cost position. We strategically shutdown our highest cost assets to align with the declining market. We were among the last assets in the developing countries to exit and enjoyed higher prices (on a small volume) than we would ever had anticipated. At the same time, we were diligently working to accelerate the industry's move to more environmentally friendly products. We were leaders in innovative products and technologies, and we encouraged customers to shift to these new products—an example of solution-based selling.

Price Discounts for a Trial or New Product Introduction

Offering discounts to entice customers to try your offering may make sense but can be risky. If you do it, be clear that this is a trial price and after a specified time or volume, the price will shift to fair market price. A small free trial may be less risky; do it in exchange for performance data or an endorsement.

Minimize the use of discounts for new product penetration:

1. Start with your loyal customers; they are 50% more likely to try your new products. You likely don't need to drop price to this group.

2. Work with just a few of the top, well-respected customers in the industry. Many other customers will follow if you have an endorsement of a well-respected competitor.

Growth Rebates

Offering your large customers rebates for volume growth beyond their previous year's purchases can incentivize them to shift a larger share of their buy to you. If you are already their sole supplier, then growth rebates are not needed.

Price Discounts for High-Priced Customers

Having customers whose price is much higher than others of equal size, without a sound rationale for this difference, can destroy the relationship if uncovered. Waive price increases, or just apply a small price increase, as a slow but steady approach to bring them back into the fair price range.

Discounts for Distributors and Value-Chain Partners

Providing special price promotions for sales growth to your value-chain partners can be an effective option. For example, this can be directed to the distribution company or it can be offered only to the individual distributors sales reps. Offer the distribution company a slightly higher commission (or greater discount) on select products you prefer they sell over other products. Offer the distributor reps a gift card for months they exceed X units of sale.

You now have the comprehensive skills for price negotiation. Yet a winning season also requires volume growth. *How do you grow your business without using price as your primary lever?* Play 4 will put you back on offense—running for volume without having your quarterback (think 'price') sacked.

Play 3:
Skill Drills to Build Your Game Plan

1. List your largest ten customers and identify the buyer type of each customer.

2. Examine the prices of these top ten customers, relative to similar-sized customers buying the same product across your entire business. Assess whether any of these appear to have lower price than expected given their buyer type (i.e., relationship buyers and value buyers should be in the middle or upper tier of prices).

3. For your largest one to three products, determine the reactive price/volume trade-off break-even percentage volume assuming you would need to drop price 10% due to competitive pressure.

4. Evaluate your pricing power for five customers—presuming they pressure you for price reductions—by thinking through the price-drop decision guideline key questions. With which of these customers might you be able to hold or increase price? With which customers might you be vulnerable to lose volume if you held or increased price?

5. Using the price-drop guidelines, formulate talking points for your top one to three toughest price negotiations that are upcoming.

    a. Assess your pricing power and whether you should consider providing price relief.

    b. Develop your talking points to these customers.

6. Map your top 10–20 customers into a customer attractiveness matrix.

    a. Determine the top attributes where you are advantaged and those you are disadvantaged in the eyes of this customer base.

    b. Set your criteria for distinguishing which customers are highly attractive to your business.

    c. Place your customers into the appropriate quadrant.

7. Set at least three policies or tactics for each quadrant of your customer attractiveness matrix.

8. What actions or behaviors will you, or your business, do differently going forward?

PLAY 4: THE SKILLS FOR BALANCING VOLUME, CUSTOMER LOYALTY, AND PRICE GROWTH

Businesses and sales organizations are tasked to both grow their volume and improve their price, often in mature markets. That makes for a tough game to win. Far too often businesses sacrifice one for the other. However, it doesn't need to be that way.

In football the best players cross-train in other sports that have the side benefit of enhancing their football performance; weightlifting or yoga, as examples. In the business world, when you cross-train in skills to increase volume without using low price as a way to 'buy' share, you not only grow but you eliminate excessive discounting. Additionally, when you create value, as a means of earning this higher share, you enhance your ability to achieve a price premium.

Creating value through innovative products can be a multiyear approach, and some businesses don't have the resources or the budget to take this approach. However, improving your customer experience to build customer loyalty is a very effective, practical way to grow both share *and* price premiums. It can distinguish you in the market; something that is vitally important in commoditized markets. The sales organization is a key contributor—often the top con-tributor—to impacting the customer experience and thus this is a growth strategy worth your consideration.

Adopting a pragmatic best practice growth strategy framework—one that builds on your strengths, identifies and busts through your barriers, as well as considers every step in the buying process, can aid you in developing effec-tive non-price oriented growth strategies.

Chapter 12:
Customer Loyalty and Price

Customer loyalty and price are often thought of as an oxymoron but they are not; you can have both. There is a wide base of evidence supporting this. Let's set the stage with one of my favorite quotes:

"If you think you lost your last sale on price, you're probably wrong. If you think you'll win your next sale by lowering your price, you're probably wrong. And even if your customer told you that you lost the last deal on price, and hinted that you could win the next sale on price, you'll probably still be wrong if you think it's about price." Charles Green[6]

Buyers will tell you it is all about price. It's not only the easy answer, it's the one that serves them best. If you believe them, you are likely to lower your price the next time. It probably will not work. The customer will likely continue to buy from the supplier that provides them the value for which they are comfortable, yet they will use your lower-price offer to pressure their preferred supplier.

If it is not about price, what is it about? Numerous B2B studies have shown that customer loyalty results in impressive volume, price, and profit gains. The findings by the Corporate Executive Board (CEB) are among the most extensive:[7]

- 14% higher retention

- 31% higher share of wallet (a combination of share and better priced accounts)

- 43% higher portfolio penetration

- 50% higher new product penetration

This loyalty is driven by creating value for the customer. How that value is typically generated is eye-opening. CEB found the following value drivers of loyalty:[8]

- Purchase experience: 53% of the time

- Brand & reputation: 19% of the time

- Product & service: 19% of the time

- Value/price ratio: 9% of the time.

When I first saw this data, I was shocked. Imagine 53% from the purchase experience! Yet as we implemented customer loyalty across the diverse DuPont businesses, in every region of the world, we found similar results in both the drivers of customer loyalty and the benefits of loyalty.

Based on our DuPont experience supplemented by additional price insights from my non-DuPont clients, Figure 12.1 shows the benefits of loyal customers over average customers.

Figure 12.1. Benefits of Loyal Customers Versus Average Customers

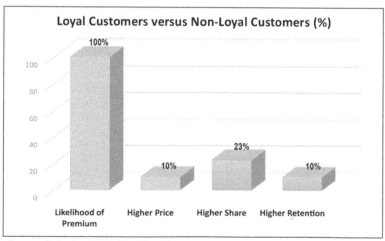

Source: DuPont and P2P Client Experience

The DuPont Customer Loyalty Experience

In 2007, DuPont set a corporate objective requiring all business units to begin measuring customer satisfaction and implementing improvement processes. At the time, only a few businesses had a strong customer-centric culture or even measured customer satisfaction. We adopted the Net Promoter Score (NPS), company-wide, as our loyalty metric. Our baseline score was modestly higher than the average B2B business. However, there was a large variation among our businesses from world class performance to others that were underperforming the B2B average. This variance provided great insights on the practices and behaviors uniquely exhibited in the business with high loyalty.

Our first year was spent implementing a survey system and gathering baseline data across the globe. By our second year, we were beginning to get traction with more businesses embracing a customer-centric culture. Yet managing through the challenges of the fourth quarter 2008/ 2009 recession slowed our progress. That all changed late in 2009. By this time, my team had gathered significant profitability and growth trend data as well as sufficient NPS data to build a compelling case for change. At DuPont's 2010 leadership meeting, we got the approval to embrace customer loyalty as a key growth and profitability driver for the company.

The Compelling Case for Change

Approximately 75% of our businesses believed they had lost product differentiation over the past decade as competitors closed the value gap. On average, our once high price premiums had declined roughly ten percentage points. Along with our product differentiation eroding, we were facing significant low-priced imports (9% in our industry sectors), predominantly from China. These combined factors contributed to a roughly 10% share decline across our businesses. This data was eye opening for leadership. *We had been growing volume and improving our profitability—how could this be?*

Fortunately, our pricing efforts, new product innovations, expansions into new markets, and other improvements were off-setting and hiding these underlying issues. We had a strategy to grow through innovation—a cornerstone of DuPont's success. However, innovation is a long-term strategy and while exciting new products were being introduced year-after-year, the lion's share of our business came from existing products. Leadership agreed that in addition to a key focus on market-driven innovation (a long-term strategy), we would focus on creating a "preferred-customer experience" (a short-term strategy).

Our NPS data, gathered from over 5000 customers, began to tell an interesting story.

Price Not a Key Loyalty Driver

Our data demonstrated that price was not a key driver in our loyalty—our loyalty score did not correlate with our price increases. As an example, our loyalty rose 30% after the 2009 recession at a time when we were implementing significant increases. As Figure 12.1 shows, loyal customers had a 10% higher price on average—the range was from 3% to 20% higher. This premium occurred in both specialty and commoditized businesses. In fact, our three businesses with the highest customer loyalty rating (at or close to world class levels) were commoditized businesses and they were among the DuPont businesses with the highest price increases. One of these businesses had increased price over 20% in one year and still retained a world-class loyalty score.

While we had price-sensitive customers, rarely did price drive loyalty or dissatisfaction. In Figure 12.2, you will notice that only 11% of customers mentioned price as a key driver.

Some of these were actually delighted with the price while the largest segment of these customers were still satisfied with DuPont; they were moderately likely to repurchase from us.

Figure 12.2. Percentage of Customers Mentioning Price in Customer Loyalty Surveys

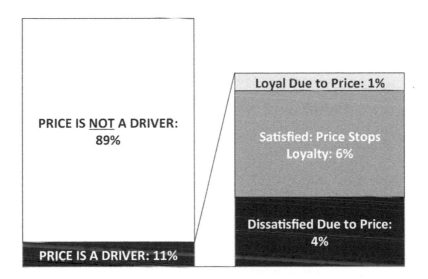

Given that price is the easiest answer (as well as self-serving) for a customer to give for not being willing to recommend us, such a low mention of price was a pleasant surprise. After years of strong price increases, our businesses worried they had been crossing the line on pushing price too hard. They had not; customers recognized the fairness in our price moves and respected the way we went about our price changes.

Not surprisingly, the bulk of the price-dissatisfied customers came from our price buyer segments. *Were they really dissatisfied with the price or was this just part of their game to position for future price negotiations?* We will never know but it is telling that their retention rate was reasonably high and the bulk of their peers didn't list price as a reason for dissatisfaction.

Customer Experience a Key Loyalty Driver

Customer experience emerged as our highest driver of both loyalty and dissatisfaction in both our specialty businesses and our commoditized product lines. Our initial data showed the following:

- Specialty product line loyalty driver: ~50% from the customer experience

- Commoditized product line loyalty driver: ~60% from the customer experience

- Dissatisfaction driver: Customer experience dominated the reason for dissatisfaction in 90% of the businesses.

We defined our customer experience as the purchasing experience (i.e., responsiveness, relationships and communications), services, and reliability. Responsiveness, relationships, and reliability were the key sub-elements of the experience that drove the greatest loyalty. The non-customer experience elements of innovation and price were not key drivers of loyalty.

Many sales teams identified highly-dissatisfied customers (NPS ratings of 0–3) and proactively worked with them to improve the situation. These highly disgruntled customers were almost always associated with a non-price complaint. In one case, a customer was so impressed with DuPont's responsiveness to their concerns they awarded us more share.

NET PROMOTER SCORE DEFINED

NPS is arguably the best measure of customer loyalty. It is based on asking customers, "Would you recommend us to a colleague? Why or Why not?"

- High responses of 9 or 10 are considered loyal—likely to repurchase and advocate on your behalf.

- Scores of 7 or 8 are considered neutral or satisfied—moderately likely to repurchase.

- Scores of 0 through 6 are considered dissatisfied—a retention risk.

The percentage of responses from dissatisfied customers are subtracted from the percentage from loyal responses. Thus, your NPS score can swing from 100% to a negative 100%. The B2B typical score is under 10%, while world class is 50% or higher.

The CEB studies found loyalty for decision makers and buyers was driven predominately by suppliers gaining widespread support from the customer's users or key influencers. They also found that loyalty for users was driven by the following top customer experience elements:[9]

- helping to quantify financial value

- being easy to buy from

- teaching valuable insights that help customers see & solve their problems, avoid landmines, and/or provide valuable perspectives on the customer's market

Using Customer Loyalty Data to Guide Price Decisions

Good customer loyalty data can help dispel the myth *you are gaining share and loyalty due to price and you are losing share due to price*. The NPS measurement forces the customer to select only the top one or two key drivers of loyalty or dissatisfaction—allowing you to focus on the most effective drivers. With other forms of customer satisfaction surveys, it can be hard to distinguish the few key drivers of your success (or failure) from the many comments.

Your customer survey responses can easily be separated into categories. In DuPont, these categories consistently emerged:

- Product

- Responsiveness

- Relationship

- Delivery and supply

- Technical support

- Price

- Innovation

- Communications

NPS data is especially valuable when you analyze your data by segment—market segments and customer needs-based segments. With less than 10% of customers citing price as a key driver, it gives confidence to the sales force that their price, in general, is not too high. Yet, analyzing your data by segment helps you uncover the groups where price sensitivity might be issue.

Questions to ask when evaluating your data should include:

- **Loyal Customer Segment**: *What are the top few drivers of loyalty? Are they the same for each market segment or for different buyer types? Do I have more value than I realized and if so, how do I get this message into my value selling tools? Are there segments that have higher value for us and if so, should I shift my customer mix towards these segments? Should I increase my price with these groups?*

- **Dissatisfaction Customer Segment**: *What are the top few drivers of dissatisfaction? Are they the same for each market segment or for different buyer types? Are there segments that are dissatisfied due to non-price issues such that if I fix these issues, I can minimize discounting? Which segments seem most price sensitive? Can I shift my customer mix away from these segments? Can I limit my discounting only to the dissatisfied segments or segments where price is the key driver of dissatisfaction?*

- **Neutral or Satisfied Segment**: *What are the top few drivers of dissatisfaction? Are they the same for each market segment or for different buyer types? If I improve my performance in the areas of dissatisfaction, can I turn some of these customers into loyal promoters? Which segments target price as the reason they are satisfied but not delighted? Could I assume that my price is likely at or close to the right price for these segments?*

This analysis will improve your confidence in pricing while highlighting other value-enhancing levers to drive loyalty.

How to Build Customer Loyalty

Building customer loyalty takes real dedication and commitment. You can make relatively fast short term gains yet a multiyear journey is needed to reap the full benefits. It takes a cultural change from leadership through sales, customer service, technical service, and even your manufacturing group. However, it is worth it, especially if you don't have a unique product to drive loyalty. A customer-focused organization centers around six behaviors and characteristics:

1. Strategy, culture, and leadership
2. Customer insights
3. Preferred-customer experience
4. Customer-centric people
5. Disciplined process
6. Visible customer metrics

Strategy, Culture, and Leadership

Creating a customer-focused organization must be driven from the top. It needs to be grounded in the strong belief that an enhanced customer experience will be rewarded with greater growth, higher prices and a competitive advantage. 'Improving the customer experience' must be a core strategy and top priority. You need a passion for (1) helping customers win and (2) getting rewarded for it. Building trust and integrity with customers is a building block. Creating experiences and solutions that help them be more successful is the target.

Visible, passionate leaders must be advocates and crusaders for the change. They must encourage and inspire their organizations. They must lead through example. Their commitment should be evident in their words during formal and informal meetings as well as in their actions and the people they reward. Additionally, it should be evident in the time they take to engage with your customer's leaders.

Customer Insights

Helping customers win requires a deep understanding of your customers and their markets. It requires asking probing questions about the customer's business such as *"Where is your business going in two to five years? What are your biggest challenges?"* and *"How are we doing as your supplier?"*. It also requires deeper analysis; loyalty/retention driver analysis, customer benefits analysis, and lost customer 'exit' interviews. These ongoing insights allow you to design the right customer experience, refine it over time, and intervene if things are not going as planned. Marketing, with sales input, should be gathering and analyzing these insights by segment, then designing the preferred-customer experience for targeted segments.

Preferred-Customer Experience

Building loyalty, goes well beyond just being nice and responsive to customers. It involves purposefully designing a unique customer experience that delivers benefits to the customer beyond the product. This experience must be designed down through all key customer touch points (e.g., every person or department that touches the customer such as sales, customer service, shipping, billing, etc.). Your organization must deliver on this experience while your marketing and sales collateral must reinforce the experience.

Challenge the Customer: The most powerful customer experiences teach new insights to your customers that help them win in their markets—insights which help them run their operations more efficiently or compete better. These insights should challenge the customer—guiding them to think in new ways which lead to a solution that you are uniquely positioned to provide. Pushing customers out of their comfort zone and into solutions that will help them win in their markets can be a powerful way to garner loyalty.[10] Telling customers what they want to hear generally will not help them win long term. Telling them something they need to hear (even if uncomfortable for them to hear) then following up with a solution can be a winning strategy. For example, throughout this book I have stated that if your growth strategy is to lower price to gain share, it is likely a profit-destroying strategy. For those of you who rely on price to grow, that can be a troubling, uncomfortable thought. However, I provide alternative strategies in Play 4. The most successful salespeople are *'challengers'*, not relationship builders.[11]

One last point on challenging the customer— *push price*. Don't apologize for your price. Be confident you have earned your price through your delivered value.

Customer-centric people

A superior experience requires you to know which functions or customer touchpoints have the greatest impact on your ability to deliver on your experience promise. You train, measure, reward, and recognize these people, whether through formal or informal systems, aligned with the designed customer experience.

Training your customer-facing resources on handling difficult customer conversations or complaints can be huge. The way your company handles upset or disgruntled customers goes a long way to customer satisfaction. Handled poorly, you might not only lose the customer, but this customer is also likely to share their grievance story to anyone who will listen. Handled well, delight the customer, and you can actually strengthen the relationship. Most of us can think of personal experiences that validate this concept. For me, it's with airlines. Over the past decade, I have avoided traveling with two airlines based on how poorly and disrespectfully they each handled a complaint. In both cases, they took a bad customer experience and made it worse in their handling of the situation. At times, I find myself delayed in airports, and inevitably a fellow passenger begins talking about other bad flying experiences. It's not long before I start sharing my own horror stories about these two airlines. On the other hand, I have my favorite airline and I am not shy about telling others that I think this airline is by far the best U.S. based airline.

Disciplined process

Creating, as well as consistently delivering, a preferred customer experience requires significant attention. It is essential to assign a leader—one with sufficient time to devote to this effort— to facilitate the cultural change, implement and oversee the process, and enable the preferred-customer experience.

Your process should include ongoing gathering of customer insights and data, analyzing this data for immediate actions as well as refinements to your designed customer experience, reporting key findings to sales and other affected functions and initiating corrective action as needed.

The marketing group typically owns systemic analyses that guide your designed customer experience. Sales, in addition to being the primary deliverer of the experience, should also contact dissatisfied customers (identified in your surveys) to resolve their concerns. Pricing should routinely use insights to inform their decisions. Operations or other affected organizations should utilize insights tied to their performance.

Visible customer metrics

Consider these metrics:

- **NPS (or equivalent) at a segment level:** Consider market segment views as well as buyer-type views. Analyze down to the root causes of loyalty and dissatisfaction.

- **Touchpoint metrics:** Measure the touchpoints' performance on elements that are key to your designed experience such as on-time delivery, number of customer service calls answered in X minutes, number of calls to resolve a customer issue, satisfaction with each order…

- **Customer retention:** Track your retention rate. For lost customers, call the customer to discover the reasons they left. If the reason is price, probe deeper. Price is usually the easy answer but rarely the real reason.

- **New Customers:** Track the number of new customers gained.

If improving your customer loyalty interests you, I would recommend reading *Value Merchants* by Anderson, Kumar and Narus, *The Ultimate Question* by Fred Reichheld, or *Chief Customer Officer* by Jeanne Bliss, in addition to *The Challenger Sale*.

Chapter 13:
Growing Volume and Price

How can you grow with a strategy that doesn't rely on using price? If the price lever is off the table, there are still a number of effective ways to grow volume. Building customer loyalty is just one of many options.

Before exploring these other options, think about your business's growth strategy. *Is it something like grow share 5%, expand volume by 10%, or be number 1 in our market?* These are not strategies. They are aspirations. They say nothing about how to go about achieving these goals. Unfortunately, for many sales organizations, that is all the guidance they are given so their go-to strategy is almost always drop price to grow share. This doesn't need to be, nor should it be, this way. Your business, marketing and/or sales leadership owe it to the sales force to provide a realistic growth strategy for sales to implement. They also owe it to the business and their stakeholders, for without a well-thought out growth strategy, profits are destined to be sub-optimized.

✗ Building a Growth Strategy—The Framework

This framework (shown in Figure 13.1) works for building either a growth strategy or a pricing strategy. It is best led by the sales and marketing leaders for the entire business, yet it can also be used by salespeople for their territory.

1. Set your goal.

2. Identify your top favorable dynamics.

3. Identify your top barriers.

4. Set strategies and tactics to take advantage of favorable dynamics or overcome barriers.

Figure 13.1. The Strategy Framework

Step 1. The Goal: Top leaders typically set the goal. Examples include 3% share gain or 10% volume growth.

Step 2. Your Favorable Dynamics: Brainstorm your top favorable dynamics which you might take advantage of to drive growth. Think of favorable features within your brand/ reputation, product, service or customer experience. Consider your internal capabilities such as being good at innovation, application development, or marketing. Keep in mind favorable industry wide dynamics such as market growth, the profitability of the customer base, and whether competitors are exiting the market or less focused on segments that interest you. *Are there gaps in the buying process that no one is taking advantage of today; ones you might position to take advantage of?* Try to come up with at least three to five dynamics yet avoid an endless list.

Step 3. Your Biggest Barriers: Brainstorm your top barriers to achieving your goal. Identify the deal breakers—the ones that must be overcome for you to get at meaningful growth.

Divide the issues between those that can be solved short-term and those that require a multi-year approach.

Consider these potential issues when identifying barriers:

- Your offering and its perceived value proposition: products, services or the customer experience

- Your brand and reputation

- Your internal capabilities or restrictions: the lack of certain skills or manpower, insufficient marketing or research and development, inadequate capital budget, the lack of support from your operations or management team, your culture, etc.

- Your external challenges: misconceptions about the market needs, a declining market, aggressive competitors, a fragmented market, customers lacking awareness of your business, insufficient products or value proposition, weak market reach, etc.

Customer Buying Process: Think through the five stages of the customers' buying process—to stretch your thinking—as you consider your barriers as well as your favorable dynamics.

1. **Need Recognition or Initiation of Purchase:**
- *Who identifies the need to purchase?*
- *What problem or opportunity are they trying to fill?*
- *Are there segments that don't recognize they have a problem or opportunity?*

2. **Identifying Potential Suppliers:**
- *Are you being considered as a supplier? As the preferred supplier?*
- *Can customers find you or can you find them?*
- *Is your brand or reputation sufficient to be selected for evaluation?*
- *Who does the search for supply and how? Are there influencers to the search?*

3. Evaluation of Suppliers:

- *How well do you stack up against other suppliers in the eyes of the customer?*
- *Is your value proposition strong and is it known and believed by customers?*
- *Does your value extend to the customer's customers? If so, is there downstream pull for you or are downstream customers pulling for another supplier?*
- *Are the users or decision makers advocates for you?*
- *How is the evaluation done (e.g., trials, proposals...)?*

4. Purchase Decision:

- *Do you offer high value for a reasonable price?*
- *Are there segments likely to value your offering/price over other segments?*
- *Are you easy and fast to do business with?*
- *Who makes the final purchase decision? Are there key influencers? Are they likely to advocate for you?*
- *How frequently do customers decide not to purchase from anyone at this stage?*

5. Purchase and Use:

- *Do you deliver on your value promise?*
- *Is your customer loyalty and retention rate high? Are there customers that you lose? Are there customers that your competitors lose?*

Ideally, you should do research to quantify your customer-base percentage leakage at each stage, so you can focus on the barrier(s) at the high-gain stages. If you lose 20% of your potential customers at stage 3, yet only 5% – 10% loss at each of the other stages, focus on attaining a deep understanding of your customer base's behavior in this stage. For example, you might find that a large segment of your market uses a product trial procedure that does not favor your product. Your strategy would then focus on changing the behaviors of these companies towards adopting a trial procedure that favors you.

As you evaluate your situation, think it through for your different market or customer needs-based segments. Expand your thinking beyond your existing market—challenge yourself to think about expansion into adjacent markets and geographies.

Step 4. Set Your Strategies and Tactics: Build strategies that focus on taking advantage of your favorable dynamics while also putting strategies in place to overcome your barriers. For example, if there is a substantial portion of customers not being called on for lack of a sufficient sales force, consider a strategy to add salespeople, telemarketing resources, or an online sales channel. Your tactics might be something such as adding two telemarketers by June 15.

Quite likely, your strategies and tactics should be aimed at targeted segments (i.e., market, customer needs-based, or geographical segments). Identifying these segments, then differentially treating and investing in them, is a key part of a good strategy.

This framework provides you a cohesive story to bring to management for their buy-in. Summarize the goal, key favorable dynamics, top barriers, strategies, and key tactics on one to two pages maximum. If management isn't convinced, you are well positioned to have a constructive discussion:

- *Do you agree with the favorable dynamics and the barriers?*

- *If not, how do you see them? (Once you are aligned on these, the rest becomes easier.)*

- *What ideas would you suggest for taking advantage of the favorable dynamics or busting the key barriers?*

Let's review a case study linked to both volume and price gain.

Case Study 13.1:

An equipment business sells through a distribution channel who sells to installers who, in turn, sell to the end-user or consumer. They used the strategy framework to set their pricing strategy while maintaining or growing share.

- *Goal: Significantly improve price increase success without jeopardizing—and possibly improving— share.*
- *Favorable Dynamics:*
  - *They are one of the largest share suppliers with a slightly better brand reputation and offering than competitors.*
  - *They have a strong and loyal installer base nurtured through training and loyalty programs.*
- *Barriers:*
  - *Unlike the installer base, the distributors don't perceive the value to themselves in selling this higher-priced product line.*
  - *The distributors struggle to sell their products at the premium price it deserved; they don't have the know-how to sell the supplier's value.*
  - *The distributor base, by and large, sells on price; they are not savvy value or price sellers.*
- *Strategies:*
  - *Develop a loyalty program for the top distributors similar to what they had done so well with their installer base.*
  - *Offer price training as well as product-value training for key national distributors.*

Strategy Examples for Volume Growth without Price Drop

Below are examples of typical barriers and favorable dynamics, listed by buying process stage, with possible high-level strategies. While not meant to be comprehensive, it can stimulate ideas for earning growth without the need to default to low price. Think of a low-price strategy as a band-aid when you really need stitches or even surgery.

Figure 13.2. Strategy Thought Starters for Favorable Conditions or Barriers

Buying Process: Overall		
Driver	Issue or Opportunity	Possible strategies
Barrier	No growth strategy	Develop marketing skills, segment & target groups most likely to buy from you, hire consulting firm…
Barrier	Very competitive market	Explore adjacent markets/regions, add new services, use marketing experts...
Barrier	Slow growth despite good value	Develop marketing skills, understand buying process key issue points, hire salesperson from successful competitor...
Buying Process: Need Recognition		
Driver	Issue or Opportunity	Possible strategies
Favorable	Large segment no one is addressing	Target this segment for growth; evaluate what it takes to win then develop a comprehensive sales plan.
Barrier	Customers don't know they have an opportunity	Educate customer via meetings, webinars, marketing communications and/or sales collateral.
Barrier	No downstream pull for our offering	Educate downstream; meetings, industry groups, marketing colleteral...
Barrier	We don't know customer needs	Research project to learn needs, hire someone from the customer's industry
Barrier	Weak pipeline of leads	Hire 'hunter' salespeople, have booth at industry conference, hold webinars and collect participant contact information.
Barrier	Insufficient or weak sales hunting resources / skills	Improve skills through training, hiring or restructuring.

(Figure 13.2 continued on following 2 pages)

Figure 13.2. *(continued from previous page)* 212

Buying Process: Identify Suppliers		
Driver	Issue or Opportunity	Possible strategies
Favorable	Higher brand/reputation	Play up your reputation while playing on the fears of not using you; improve your marketing collateral to this end.
Favorable	Larger and better salesforce	Align sales to underperforming segments, enhance sales skills further, include benefits of better sales in marketing collateral.
Barrier	Not well known to potential customers	More advertising. Add sales or online sales channel. Hire salesperson from competitor. Present at industry forums.
Barrier	Weak brand or reputation	Branding campaigns and/or improve performance. Offer performance guarantees or warranties.
Barrier	Value proposition is not understood / believed	Quantify value and create value proposition tools or collateral. Get customer endorsements. Offer warranties.
Barrier	Not enough sales resources to cover market	Use telemarketing, hire resources or shift resources from low value segments. Add new routes to market like distribution,
Barrier	We don't know how to identify customers	Hire an experienced sales person from the industry, buy industry sales/company lists

Buying Process: Evaluate Suppliers		
Driver	Issue or Opportunity	Possible strategies
Favorable	Better value	Improve value selling collateral and selling skills
Barrier	No product or service differentiation	Innovate, create a unique customer experience or a unique value proposition.
Barrier	Our value proposition only fits a niche market	Develop an extended offering to fit other segment needs. Offer choices. Acquire a company to fill out your offering.
Barrier	Price too high for the value to some segments	Develop a low price, low cost offering. Add a web channel offering.
Barrier	Sales lack good product knowledge	Educate sales on products and their value. Provide easy to use selling materials and tools.
Barrier	Competitor A is preferred supplier in segment X	Focus on segment Y. Position as strong secondary supplier for segment X in the short term. Develop a stronger value
Barrier	Our company or offering is not well known.	Offer free trials, provide warranties or guarantees, quantify value... customer endorsements or case studies.

Figure 13.2. Strategy Thought Starters for Favorable Conditions or Barriers
(continued from previous page)

Buying Process: Purchase Decision		
Driver	Issue or Opportunity	Possible strategies
Favorable	Tight supply/demand	Consider customer or product mix enrichment, raise price...
Favorable	Higher internal costs	Raise price.
Favorable	Competitors increasing price	Raise price.
Barrier	Weak sales negotiation skills	Train sales on sales & price negotiation, create loyalty programs (e.g., frequent buyer perks)...
Barrier	Customers use multiple suppliers	Offer growth rebates for volume above previous year's purchases.
Barrier	Poor close rate	Better prequalify deals, pre-sell to users or decision makers, train sales on sales & price negotiation, offer free trials...
Buying Process: Buy and Use		
Driver	Issue or Opportunity	Possible strategies
Favorable	Better value and customer experience	Upsell or raise price, build deeper relationships, quantify value or get endorsements.
Barrier	Mature or declining market	Expand into adjacent markets/regions, reduce services, shutdown any unneeded, high-cost assets.
Barrier	Poor retention	Build customer focused culture, measure/analyze loyalty & causes of poor retention.

Play 4:
Skill Drills to Build Your Game Plan

1. If you were to design the 'preferred customer experience' for your company to engender loyalty—what would that experience look like?

2. How far off is your designed customer experience from your customer's current experience? Is it practical to close this gap? Is it worth the effort?

3. What are your current sales goals for volume and price? What are your current strategies to achieve these goals?

4. What are the top three favorable dynamics or drivers in your business which can be built upon to improve price and/or volume?

5. What are your top three challenges or barriers in growing business?

6. Does the current growth strategy build upon your strengths and overcome your key challenges? If not, are there other strategies to consider?

7. What actions or behaviors will you, or your business, do differently going forward?

Epilogue:
Pulling it all together

You now have the skills and the toolkit you need to negotiate price with confidence and conviction (see Table E.1.).

⚒ **Table E.1.** Price Negotiation Toolbox

Price Negotiation ToolKit		
Tools	Play	Chapter
1. Behavior Guidelines for Influencing the market	1,2 & 3	1, 4 & 7
2. Price/Volume Trade-off Tables: Proactive & Reactive	1 & 3	2 & 7
3. Value Quantification	2	3
4. Price Increase Communication Guidelines	2	4
5. Negotiation Planning Checklist	2	5
6. Price Increase Pulse Check Meetings	2	5
7. Buyer Type Identification Summary	3	6
8. Buyer Type Policies and Tactics Summary	3	6
9. Customer Attractiveness Matrix: Mapping & Policies	3	7
10. Price Drop Decision Guidelines	3	9
11. Price and Non-Price Alternatives to Discounting	3	9
12. Price Pressure Negotiation Framework	3	10
13. Buyer Qualification Checklist	3	10
14. Negotiation Tips for Enhanced Influence	3	10
15. Strategy Framework for Growth or Price Gain	4	13

You know your pricing power and you can begin to use it to its fullest. To use a football analogy—each salesperson can advance the ball toward the goal line, yet it's when the entire team is engaged that touchdowns and big wins occur. Getting your team on board is important, but don't wait for this to happen before you begin using your new skills. Partial success is far better than no success.

Overtime, as you consistently practice this disciplined approach you will reduce price aggression in your industry. Customers and competitors will sense a change in your approach and it will impact their own behaviors.

If you would like to discuss any portion of this book, feel free to connect with me at www.price2profits.com or www.linkedin.com/in/smithjoannem/. I am humbled that you invested the time to learn these approaches and tools. I wish you great success as you begin to apply these concepts.

You've got this. Go team go!

NOTES

1. Christian Homburg, *Perceived Pricing Position Study* (University of Mannheim, *2010*).

2. Simon-Kucher & Partners, *2016 Global Pricing Study* (simon-kucher.com). http://www.simon-kucher.com/en/about/media-center/global-pricing-study-2016-every-second-company-involved-price-war-0.

3. "Prisoner's Dilemma," *Wikipedia*," last modified January 24, 2018, https://en.wikipedia.org/wiki/Prisoner%27s_dilemma.

4. LeveragePoint, *Transforming Case Studies into Digital Value Propositions*, (leveragePoint.com). https://www.leveragepoint.com/

5. Simon-Kucher & Partners, 2012 Global Pricing Study (simon-kucher.com).

6. Charles H. Green, *The Dirty Truth About Pricing* (Trusted Advisor,2010) http://trustedadvisor.com/public/files/pdf/articles/2010TheDirtyTruthAboutPrice.pdf.

7. Corporate Executive Board, Marketing & Sales Council, 2007 (CEB presentation to DuPont 2008).

8. Matthew Dixon and Brent Adamson, *The Challenger Sale* (Corporate Executive Board, Sales Leadership Council, 2011), 47.

9. Dixon and Adamson, *The Challenger Sale, 107*

10. Dixon and Adamson, *The Challenger Sale, 107*.

11. Dixon and Adamson, *The Challenger Sale, 22*.

Acknowledgments

Many people have supported, inspired, or taught me as I have developed my own pricing competency. They have contributed to the pricing success of both the DuPont company and my Price to Profits Consulting clients.

I especially want to thank the business and sales leaders who took a leap of faith—in very competitive markets—to embrace my (or my team's) bold pricing recommendations. Without their courage and leadership, I would not have been able to refine the practices shared in this book nor provide you, the reader, with the success stories that no doubt helps to build your confidence in making your own bold moves.

These leaders come from both my P2P clients—leaders such as Dirk Hoelher, Hans Detlef Luginsland, Michael Ruebenkoenig, Richard Reif, Chris Mooney, Matt Mears, and Harold Dodd, as well as from within DuPont—leaders such as Keith Smith, Tim McCann, BC Chong, Bill Weber, Rick Olsen, Barry Owens, Peter O'Sullivan, Craig Binetti, Marsha Craig, and Michelle Fite (to name just a few).

I owe a debt of gratitude to the courageous leaders who initially persuaded DuPont to create a corporate marketing and sales organization, with a special emphasis on pricing. They provided me the opportunity to be among the key players in leading the pricing and marketing transformation of DuPont. These leaders included Diane Gulyas, John Hodgson, Mahesh Mansukhani, and William White.

I owe a special heartfelt thanks to the key leaders and thought partners on my DuPont pricing and customer loyalty teams: Todd Freeman, Meena Panchapaksan, Neil Bunis and Jane Clampitt for their groundbreaking leadership. Many other pricing-resource people contributed significantly to

DuPont's success, and I thank them. Also a special thanks to Dan James, former Corporate Sales Director, for his partnership and successful efforts at enhancing the sales force competency. Dan continues to inspire me as well as share his wealth of knowledge on sales effectiveness.

Many external firms contributed to my development and success in the area of price execution. I particularly acknowledge the Professional Pricing Society and The Monitor Group (now part of Deloitte)—Thomas Nagle, John Hogan, and Lisa Thompson.

Lastly, a number of people supported me, inspired me or guided me in the writing of this book. First and foremost, my editor, Jeanne Marie Blystone, for her dedication, patience and great advice. Bill Blystone and John Blystone, my editor's husband and son as well as superb lifelong sales leaders, for suggestions to this book. Keith Smith, former DuPont and SABIC Executive, for his pragmatic advice. My good friend, former DuPont sales professional, Sharon Gidumal, as well as Anne Lewis, Pricing Leader at SABIC for their suggestions and additions to this book. Special thanks to Tim McCann for his thoughtful additions.

About the Author

Joanne Smith's passion, purpose, and power lie in managing change within organizations to transform their capabilities for superior results. During her career spanning three decades, she was fortunate to work with enlightened leaders who had the courage to embrace change on a large scale.

Coming in on the creation of DuPont's Corporate Marketing and Sales organization, Joanne became its global head of marketing and pricing. For more than six years, she drove pricing excellence, customer loyalty, and marketing effectiveness at DuPont. Through her extensive success with DuPont and her Price to Profits Consulting clients, she was able to "write the playbook" for future sales teams facing similar challenges. As a teacher for the Professional Pricing Society and their certified pricing program, Joanne often teaches courses focused on the best practices for price execution, advanced strategic pricing, value-based pricing, and transforming a company's price competency. She is also the author of *"The Price and Profit Playbook: A Practical and Strategic Guide to Generating Superior Profits Based on DuPont's Success"*.

Beginning her career at DuPont as a chemical engineer, Joanne first worked in and managed chemical manufacturing plants. For close to 30 years, DuPont tapped into her abilities in a variety of leadership roles, including business and product line management, as well as directing the company's adoption of the rigorous Six Sigma methods for process improvement.

Attaining superior results has always been the "goal line" for this innovative leader and pricing expert. Today, Joanne runs Price to Profits Consulting, a consulting firm that assists B2B companies in transforming their pricing performance to enhance long-term profitability. She teaches pricing courses, as well as provides keynote speeches, around the world. Joanne resides in Avondale, Pennsylvania.

Price to Profits Consulting, LLC
(http://www.price2profits.com)

info@price2profits.com

Phone 484-459-0166

joannesmith@price2profits.com or
joanne.m.smith122@gmail.com